Florida's ANTEBELLUM HOMES

Florida's ANTEBELLUM HOMES

LEWIS N. WYNNE AND JOHN T. PARKS

Frontispiece: The log cabin was a familiar site for visitors to antebellum Florida. (Florida State Archives.)

ISBN 0-7385-1617-1

Published by Arcadia Publishing
Charleston SC, Chicago IL, Portsmouth NH, San Francisco CA

Printed in Great Britain

Library of Congress Catalog Card Number: 2004100459

For all general information contact Arcadia Publishing at:
Telephone 843-853-2070
Fax 843-853-0044
E-Mail sales@arcadiapublishing.com

For customer service and orders:
Toll-Free 1-888-313-2665

Visit us on the internet at http://www.arcadiapublishing.com

Contents

Acknowledgments

There are always a lot of people to thank when authors finally see a book in print. A book is always a collaborative effort—the work of many people—and, unfortunately, authors always seem to miss listing some of the most important contributors. John Parks and I sincerely thank those people who helped. In order to avoid missing someone, we have decided not to list individuals. That way, no one can complain.

We do want to mention institutions, however. Florida is extremely lucky—at least for now—to have an active and competent group of individuals working in the State Historical Preservation Bureau. The individuals in the Site File collection were particularly helpful in making this book possible. So, too, were the staffers in the Florida State Archives Photographic Collection—thank you. The staff at the Alma Clyde Field Library of History in Historic Cocoa Village provided a number of photographs and much advice, and we would like to thank them as well.

The mistakes in this work are to be placed on the authors. Credit should go to the entire Florida historical community.

This book is dedicated to my wife, Debra, who always enthusiastically supports my projects,
and to my children, Patrick and Lisa. —Nick Wynne
To my wife, Marjorie, and my mother, Patricia, who both have encouraged my professional efforts
in the fields of historical research and historic preservation. —John Parks

Introduction

Florida has sometimes been referred to as the "most Southern of the Northern states" of the United States, while others have referred to it as the "most Northern of the Southern states." Much of this comes from the fact that almost 85 percent of the state's current population comes from somewhere else, primarily from the colder, more industrialized states of the Midwest and Northeast. The earliest Spanish settlers established this trend of in-migration as indigenous Native American populations dwindled, ultimately resulting in the loss of the entire original Native Americans population by 1763, when Spain turned Florida over to British authorities. As the American Revolution exploded, loyalists from the Thirteen Colonies made their way to the area and brought with them the Southern plantation system and African slavery. Although the period of British ownership was brief—a mere 20 years—the patterns of settlement and economic development of the Lower South persisted. Different from the Spanish hacienda system, the plantation system emphasized a cash-crop economy based on the institution of a permanent class of hereditary slaves.

Although control of the Florida Peninsula reverted to Spain in 1783, Spanish authorities were not able to govern this large and open region. Foreign adventurers and American filibusterers raised their flags in Spanish territory, while members of the Lower Creek nation; white yeoman farmers

from Georgia, Alabama, and the Carolinas; and runaway slaves looked to the empty spaces of the peninsula and made their way southward. The demands of plantation owners in the United States for the return of fugitive slaves and the continuing conflicts between whites and Native Americans as the American frontier pushed westward soon led to Jackson's invasion of the peninsula. Faced with the reality of limited resources to deal with American incursions and an increasingly restless Native population, Spain agreed to the Adams-Onis Treaty in 1821, which ceded Florida to the United States.

American occupation of Florida, first as a territory and after March 1845 as a state, plunged the United States into the longest and, for the time, most expensive wars in its history. Despite the upheavals of fighting three Seminole Indian Wars and the uncertainties of the geography of the largely unexplored peninsula, Americans pushed inexorably into Florida. Along the northern border between Pensacola and modern Jacksonville, southward to present-day Ocala and Palatka, large cotton, tobacco, and naval stores plantations were created out of virgin timberland. Further south, yeoman farmers and cattle ranchers moved into the vast plains of Central Florida. Fueled by the prospect of free or inexpensive land guaranteed by the Armed Occupation Act—a federal land program that promoted the idea of "fortified hamlets" as the first line of defense against the Seminoles—Florida's population began to steadily increase. By 1845, despite fierce internal political battles, Florida entered the Union as a new state.

Statehood placed Florida firmly in the fold of Southern slave states. Slave owners operated plantations, large and small, which produced approximately 90 percent of the state's wealth. This affluence, concentrated in 10 or 12 counties along the northern rim and center of Florida, secured control of the state's political system for slave owners, many of whom had close and direct family ties with the planter families in other Southern states. These familial ties, coupled with similar economic interests and the relative newness of the state's slave-based economy, produced another Florida that has been described as the "most Southern of the Southern states." By 1860 approximately 50 percent of the state's total population of 140,000 were slaves engaged in agricultural pursuits. The state's commitment to its "Southerness" was no more evident than in its decision to follow South Carolina and Mississippi into the uncharted seas of Southern independence.

Florida architecture for the antebellum period (1821–1866) reflected several major themes. First, the earlier Spanish and British influences continued to shape architecture in the established cities of Pensacola and St. Augustine. Second, the constant threat of Indian wars (1821–1857) dictated that houses on the frontier incorporate defensive features figured prominently into their design and construction, while further north, the same concerns caused some plantation owners to build their residences within the confines of small towns. Third, the close family and business ties of planters with older, more established areas of the slave South produced elaborate residences that could easily fit into the plantation architecture of South Carolina, Georgia, or Mississippi.

In *Florida's Antebellum Houses*, we will present photographic images and line drawings of Florida buildings that incorporate all or parts of these design features. In addition, we will look at some of the public buildings of the period churches, banks, hospitals, and government buildings that reflect the emerging senses of personal affluence, civic pride, and political development. Most of these buildings unfortunately no longer exist as they fell prey to natural catastrophes, unbridled expansion, and the relentless march of Florida's exacting climate. Some, however, are maintained in pristine condition and invite the general public to appreciate their beauty today as much as earlier Floridians reveled in their stateliness.

John Parks and Nick Wynne
January 2004

Chapter One

SPANISH AND BRITISH FLORIDA

The Spanish laid claim to the Florida Peninsula with its 1513 discovery by Ponce de Leon. Although Spain would not establish a permanent settlement in Florida until 1565, the demands on the Spanish government to allocate resources to more profitable colonies in Central and South America meant that even the small enclaves at St. Augustine and Pensacola were viewed as being of minimal importance to the Spanish crown. Viewed primarily as first lines of defense for treasure fleets and other colonies, Spanish Florida received little in the way of support. As a result, these two small towns, which remained stunted and underdeveloped, represented the high water mark of Spanish occupation. Even the extensive system of missions that dotted the interior of the North American continent as far north as present-day South Carolina and as far west as Mobile consisted of little more than simple churches, surrounded by small populations of indigenous people who were barely able to produce subsistence-level crops. All in all, Spanish Florida was a dismal affair, reflecting none of the grandeur of other Spanish colonies such as Mexico or Peru.

Despite its isolation and lack of attention, inhabitants of Spanish Florida did attempt to replicate some of the familiar surroundings of Spain. Festivals, social institutions, churches, and other cultural activities mimicked those of Spain. Residents of Spanish Florida also sought to duplicate the architecture of the villages of Europe, but the absence of substantial amounts of hard stone and the lack of great deposits of clay dictated that while the structures of St. Augustine and Pensacola might capture the ambiance of these villages, they lacked the substance of them.

There were few large and awe-inspiring public structures in St. Augustine, with the exception of the Castillo de San Marcos, the cathedral, and the governor's compound. These buildings pale in significance when compared to public buildings in Havana, Lima, or Mexico City. At its height, St. Augustine—and certainly Pensacola—remained little more than a rustic village of small residences, dirt streets, and small shops. Florida was little more than a colonial backwater and offered little in the way of great wealth or military prestige for professional soldiers or bureaucrats. Those unfortunate enough to draw an assignment to St. Augustine or Pensacola had to face the reality that their careers were dead in the water.

Despite its lackluster history as a part of the Spanish and British empires, Florida nevertheless fueled the imaginations of many adventurers as they considered the pleasant climate, the fertile land, and open spaces as an absolute guarantee that the real riches of the peninsula lay hidden in its vast unexplored regions. Most of the peninsula remained unexplored until United States soldiers, pursuing Seminoles and Miccosukees in the 1820s, 1830s, and 1840s, began to systematically explore and map it. Perhaps the greatest legacy of the early colonial inhabitants—both Spanish and British—was not their economic or military achievements, but their perseverance despite the absence of hope for anything but the most meager success.

The strategic locations of St. Augustine and Pensacola accounted for the willingness of the Spanish and British governments to continue their occupation of Florida even though neither government ever made a profit on the peninsula. St. Augustine managed to stave off several early invasions by British colonists from Georgia and South Carolina, while providing some protection to Spanish galleons as they traveled the Gulf Stream. The city also served as the administrative hub of the Catholic Church in Florida, although the Bishop of Havana exercised overall control.

It is understandable then that the most prominent buildings in the St. Augustine belonged either to the Spanish government and military or to the Church. Merchants who serviced the needs of these three entities prospered, although modestly, and built homes and shops of masonry, coquina rock, and wood that reflected their elevated status. Many of these houses still exist and, though heavily modified and remodeled over the centuries, remain today as tourist attractions. Although generally not classified as Southern antebellum houses, the influence of their style and construction remained as features of Florida architecture to the present.

For the lower classes, wooden houses made from locally grown timber were sufficient, and few of these have survived the ravages of weather over the almost 500 years of the city's existence. Nevertheless, these small common dwellings also had an impact on the construction of yeoman houses during the American territorial and antebellum periods.

Spanish Pensacola, like St. Augustine, remained little more than a village of several hundred hardy souls during the colonial period. Like St. Augustine, Pensacola was a military outpost, and the most prominent buildings were forts and smaller fortifications. Located in the far western part of today's Panhandle region, the town provided a bulwark against French activities along the Mississippi River and central North America. Later, Spanish authorities took comfort that the city served as a defense against the upstart Americans who replaced the French with the purchase of Louisiana. Although the city did provide some protection against unwanted intrusions, it was not unconquerable and changed hands several times.

Little growth occurred in either Pensacola or St. Augustine during the period of British control from 1763 to 1783. Great Britain, whose Indian, Asian, and African colonies produced great wealth for the motherland, used Florida primarily as a place of refuge for planters escaping possible slave revolts in the West Indies and for loyalists who faced confiscation of their property and possible loss of life during the American Revolution. The British encouraged individuals of substantial means to settle Florida, and a generous policy of granting large blocks of land did attract a few individuals and groups willing to invest in the new colony. Overall, however, British attempts to replicate the colonial economy of the West Indies proved to be a dismal failure. The single greatest economic success for the British came from the establishment of a large and lucrative trade with Native Americans.

Although small changes did occur with the introduction of life slavery and a cash crop economy of tobacco, cotton, and indigo, these changes were minor and failed to reshape Florida in any significant fashion. When control of the peninsula passed back to Spain in 1783, even these changes quickly disappeared. From 1783 until 1821, Spanish Florida remained a somnambulant colony, driven to occasional outbursts of excitement caused by American military incursions and filibustering expeditions.

During the Second Spanish Period, Florida was considered to be governed in name only by the Spanish and was generally regarded as territory ripe for the taking by Americans and others. From 1790 until 1804, Spanish authorities in Florida followed a policy of making generous land grants to Americans, who, in exchange, were required to take an oath of allegiance to the King of Spain. Several hundred Americans moved south to take advantage of this generous policy, but relationships between the authorities and the American émigrés were "iffy" at best. Tensions between the Spanish and their newest a rivals were the product of cultural differences, mixed loyalties, and a decided difference in attitudes toward Native Americans. The uneasy peace that initially accompanied the inclusion of Americans into Spanish territory sometimes exploded into violence.

In 1810 President James Madison annexed part of West Florida to Louisiana, and following communications with the governor of West Florida, he undertook, with Congressional approval, the formulation of a plan to annex the remainder of the peninsula. In 1812 self-styled American "Patriots," led by Gen. George Mathews, a former governor of Georgia, moved across the St. Marys River and occupied the territory between the St. Johns and St. Marys Rivers.

During the War of 1812, Andrew Jackson, leading an American Army Volunteers and Tennessee Militia, fought a vicious frontier war against the Creeks. In 1816 a small American invasion resulted in the destruction of the "Negro Fort" on the Apalachicola River. In 1817 a Scottish soldier-of-fortune, Gen. Gregor MacGregor, led a successful filibustering invasion of Fernandina and took the town without firing a shot. He then proclaimed the town independent of Spanish authority. The United States had officially ended the foreign slave trade in 1808, and the illegal importation of additional slaves via Fernandina drew a quick response from President James Monroe. Orders were dispatched to the U.S. Navy to deal with the situation. Monroe, reluctant to leave the port open to any future filibusterers, notified the Spanish authorities that the United States would hold the city in "protective custody" until Spain could marshal sufficient forces to control the area.

Although the continued instability of East and West Florida under the Spanish had led to talks between the Monroe administration and the Spanish government over the possibility of the United States acquiring the peninsula, events in West Florida soon led to another American invasion. At issue once again were the questions of runaway slaves and Indian incursions against plantations along the Georgia-Florida-Alabama border. President Monroe decided to send Andrew Jackson south to deal with the problem. With a force of 1,000 Tennessee militiamen, he proceeded to move down the Apalachicola River, where he erected a small fort on the site of the former Negro Fort. Faced with its inability to govern Florida and to prevent its further occupation by the United States military, Spain agreed to the Adams-Onis Treaty on February 19, 1819. With the formal ratification of the treaty by the United States Senate in 1821, Florida became an American territory.

And so ended almost 300 years of Spanish control of Florida.

The gates of St. Augustine guarded the entrance to a small, European-style village in the 1830s. Only a few hundred people lived here and walked the muddy streets during the colonial period, and the city experienced little growth during the territorial and early statehood periods. (National Archives.)

Pensacola, in 1747, was a small village of mostly wooden houses and an inadequate harbor. (Charlton Tebeau, A History of Florida.)

The fortress Castillo de San Marcos in St. Augustine was renamed Fort Marion after the American acquisition in 1821. (Alma Clyde Field Library.)

The Cathedral of St. Augustine was one of the few public buildings that attracted the attention of visitors to colonial St. Augustine.

Above: Government business for East Florida was conducted in this imposing structure during the colonial period. It was located on the north side of the town square, which also included an open-air slave market.

Right: This building was used as an open-air market for the residents of St. Augustine; slave sales were also conducted. The open sides allowed an interested person to view potential slave purchases from all sides.

Houses in St. Augustine mimicked the architectural style of European houses and those of the Caribbean.

As late as the 1860s, residents of St. Augustine still followed the Colonial style of architecture. Here, Union troops face the camera from the balcony of this house.

The Lavalle House, a frame vernacular Creole cottage, was built between 1803 and 1815 in Pensacola. It is one of the few remaining 19th-century frame houses in the city.

The Lavalle house was moved to Historic Pensacola Village in 1969 and restored.

The Panton-Leslie Trading Company was the most lucrative business to emerge in Florida during the British period, 1763–1783. This was their trading post and headquarters in Pensacola.

The Spanish governor's house in Pensacola was a simple Creole-style building located on Intendencia Street. Since no picture exists, Emma Chandler, a Pensacola resident, created this sketch from written records. (Pace Library, University of West Florida.)

Left: Andrew Jackson, bane of Spanish officials and hero to Americans, became the first American governor of Florida in 1821.

Above: This old building was the jail in Spanish Pensacola. When the Spanish governor defied Andrew Jackson, he was incarcerated until he agreed to furnish the papers the American general requested.

Chapter Two

THE COTTON KINGDOM
From Territory, Through Statehood, and into the Confederacy

The formal annexation of Florida by the United States in 1821 marked the rise of the "Cotton Kingdom" in Florida. Within a single generation, Central and North Florida, collectively referred to as "middle" Florida, had matured into a fully developed plantation area, complete with large slave holdings, a cash crop economy of cotton and tobacco, and splendid mansions. The planting elite brought with them the customs and traditions of older slaveholding areas and quickly established them in Florida. So, too, did they bring their expectations of dominating the political life of the new territory. Within a few years, the cultural, economic, and political life of Florida was indistinguishable from that of other Southern states. To a great extent, their expectations were fully met.

Even before the formal transfer of title to the United States, hardy souls had braved passage through the barren pinelands of lower central Georgia and made their way to the area. Most belonged to the lower economic class and brought little with them except a desire for land and a willingness to work hard. Settling on the best acreage, these early pioneers set about the tasks of clearing small plots and beginning subsistence agricultural operations. Poor in the main, they relied upon pooled family resources, their own labor, or that of adjacent families to achieve the Herculean goal of carving out a homestead in the

forests of North Florida. Few of the early settlers had the resources—monetary, emotional, and educational—to fight for their claims and win. Within a matter of a few years, the majority of these early settlers found themselves forced to move.

While some moved west to Alabama and beyond, a significant portion of these pioneers pushed further south into less desirable lands. Vast areas of open plains, hammocks, swamps, and thin, sandy soil fully covered 80 percent of the peninsula, and yeoman farmers and their families soon settled these areas. The disparity between the lives of the wealthy planters and those of the "countrymen" was visible as a traveler moved southward out of the rolling hills of North Florida. Small holdings, usually measured in the tens of acres or a few hundred at best, dominated the yeoman economy, and slaves, so visible on the great plantations, were seldom found. The few yeomen who could afford slaves frequently owned only one or two, and these were more likely to be treated as poor relatives than as chattel. Land alone was not a solid foundation for achieving easy wealth, and dreams of success could not be realized without prior wealth or powerful connections. While a few unusual individuals did achieve great things, the majority of the "countrymen" found life in Florida to be a day-to-day struggle for survival.

As more Americans pushed into Florida, tensions between them and the Seminoles were at a high level. The Seminoles, faced with an unstoppable onslaught of settlers, carried out sporadic raids on isolated homesteads and plantations in unsuccessful attempts to prevent further infringements on their land. Despite their efforts to halt the influx of more settlers, the Seminoles were forced to retreat further and further south.

The decision to locate the new capital of the Florida territory in Tallahassee in 1823, away from the old Spanish towns of Pensacola and St. Augustine, provided additional impetus to attract planters from the other Southern states to Florida. The attacks by the Seminoles did not stop the continued migration to Florida. In the older slave states of the Lower South, some plantation owners recognized that over-cultivation and poor agricultural practices had depleted the soil and reduced the size of cotton and tobacco harvests. Without some way to replenish the soil, the only choices left to them were to either accept a continuously declining standard of living or to uproot their families and move to new areas where the land was still productive. Sons of prominent and wealthy families who still planted successfully, realizing that little new land was available in the established areas of their states, gathered their possessions, said goodbye to family and friends, and set off to recreate the plantations societies of North Carolina, South Carolina, Georgia, and Virginia in the wilds of Florida. Indeed, some areas of the region around Tallahassee held so many settlers from a particular state that the micro-region frequently was referred to by the contributing state's name.

Although primogeniture—the legal practice of making the first son in a family the only heir—did not exist in the United States, the desire to preserve large estates frequently led to similar practices in reality. Second and third sons were encouraged to seek out new areas and settle them. Substantial gifts of slaves and money, bolstered by established credit sources, meant that these settlers could claim, clear, purchase, and put into production large tracts of land quickly. Scions of the wealthiest Southern families sometimes established multiple plantations in the same region or within a few miles of each other, which allowed them to maximize their resources and to assist each other. Within a matter of a decade, it was possible to connect Florida planters with virtually all of the prominent families of the Lower South, and names such as Gamble, Jones, Lanier, Parkhill, Randolph, Croom, Eppes, and others became commonplace.

In many ways, however, the idyllic picture of Florida in 1860 was deceiving. The great plantations were limited to a small area of the peninsula, barely seven to ten counties. By 1860, Florida had a population of 140,424 persons, and of this number, whites of all economic groups numbered 77,746 or 56 percent. The remaining 62,678 persons were slaves. Some 5,152 individuals, a mere 3.6 percent of the white population, were slave owners. Yet, this small group accounted for 71 percent of the cash value of all agricultural property in Florida. In addition, the same group owned all or parts of the major business ventures in the state, from sawmills to railroads to town development. The commercial ties between Florida planters and cotton and tobacco factors in Charleston, New Orleans, and major Northern cities also gave them access to the great lending institutions of the period. Few commercial enterprises could hope to succeed without the direct involvement of planters or, at the least, their support. Thus, strong ties between planters and businessmen in the towns were quickly developed, though planters remained atop the economic hierarchy.

Because most planters maintained residences in towns or in the immediate vicinity, such ties were further strengthened by frequent social interactions and, in some cases, by marriage. Prominent commercial leaders mimicked planters in dress, language, customs, and the architecture of their homes. In Tallahassee, for example, wealthy merchants who lived side-by-side with planters sent their children to the same schools and participated in the same social events. Some merchants also attempted to move into the planter class by purchasing land and slaves and embracing the cotton and tobacco culture. A small number of merchants made the transition successfully.

Planters were so powerful in the political life of Florida that they dominated the Secession Convention of 1861. Fully 80 percent of the delegates were classified as planters, and another 10 percent were urban allies. When the Civil War ended in 1865, the great plantations of Florida began to quickly disappear. Most eventually fell to urban development or to the eventual collapse of the cotton and tobacco markets, while others were divvied among tenant farmers and sharecroppers. Some were sold by their owners to cover debts, while still others were abandoned. Those few that remain today are preserved primarily as vacation retreats or as specialized hunting and fishing operations. Without the underpinnings of slavery and a voracious demand for cotton, plantations were black holes that sucked in scarce resources. In the words of Margaret Mitchell, they were "gone with the wind."

This cabin was typical of an early yeoman farming family in Florida. Few in number, poor in resources, and generally limited in education, these early settlers could only hope that the improvements they made to the land would be sufficient to allow them to "prove" their claims when the government of the United States imposed stringent requirements through the Florida Land Claims Commission. Few of the early settlers had the resources—monetary, emotional, and educational—to fight for their claims and win.

Since Florida was virgin land, it was necessary to clear trees, stumps, and brush for fields. An individual yeoman family might be able to clear five or ten acres a year, barely enough to sustain subsistence agriculture, while slave owners, able to bring large labor gangs of slaves to the task, cleared large tracts that were suitable for the cultivation of cotton, sugarcane, and tobacco on a commercial scale. By the 1830s, the network of planting families with ties to prominent families in other states dominated the ten counties that eventually constituted the heart of Florida's plantation district. Few individual yeomen could compete with these built-in advantages and soon left the areas of prime land.

Although early plantations were, by necessity, little more than collections of crude frontier buildings fortified against Seminole attacks, these structures were temporary at best or eventually used to house slaves or overseers. Despite bearing illustrious names like Magnolia, Tuscawilla, and Spring Hill, it was not until the end of the problems with Native Americans and the full development of the cash crop economy that they began to take on the more ostentatious appearances of later homes.

Within the short span of 40 years, Florida moved from being a crude and coarse United States territory, short on culture and dependent on subsistence agriculture, to a state (in 1845) with the veneer of a wealthy, educated, and well-developed plantation state. The rapid change was brought about by the infusion of established wealth from other states in the South and availability of prime farmlands in North and Central Florida. The importation of a planter culture into Florida was not limited to slaves or wealth; slave owners also brought with them an allegiance to the mythology of an aristocratic landed gentry, whose right to rule and to dominate society was a right of birth. During the 1850s, this mythology manifested itself in a decade of jousts, tournaments, and ritualistic "court" parties where males and females assumed roles of knights and ladies and acted out their fantasies of Walter Scott's vision of an earlier chivalric English society. Planters and their families undertook the "Grand Tour" of Europe, returning with a reinforced view of their own importance and the right of aristocrats to rule. Plantation homes were often furnished with goods bought on the continent during such tours or imported from Europe by factors eager to satisfy the desires of their customers. In this, Florida planters were no different from their counterparts in other Southern states. The Grove, pictured here, was the home of Richard Keith Call.

Although most Florida planters were in favor of protecting slavery as an institution, not all were supportive of taking the state out of the Union and joining a new confederation of slave states. Richard Keith Call, former aide to Andrew Jackson, slave owner and former territorial governor, was quite vocal in his opposition to secession. When the convention voted 62 to 5 to secede, Call angrily declared that the delegates had "opened the gates of Hell, from which shall flow the curses of the damned which shall sink you to perdition!" Despite his opposition to secession, Call and others, such as David Levy Yulee and Stephen R. Mallory, who shared his opposition were not abolitionists, hoped to find some way to protect slavery without leaving the Union. (Alma Clyde Field Library.)

David Levy Yulee, planter, politician, and entrepreneur, was a popular figure in antebellum Florida. He, like R.K. Call, opposed secession, became a reluctant Confederate, but remained loyal to regional and class interests. Above all, they remained firm in their commitment to preserve the slave system. (Alma Clyde Field Library.)

Chapter Three

PUBLIC BUILDINGS IN ANTEBELLUM FLORIDA

The first permanent capital for Florida was chosen in 1823, when John Lee Williams of Pensacola and Dr. W.H. Simmons of St. Augustine were asked by the territorial government to find a suitable location near the Ochlockonee and Suwannee Rivers. Williams and Simmons agreed that the ideal location was the site of a village occupied by Neamathla and his people. In April 1824 the first white settlers, led by John McIver of North Carolina, arrived at the new town of Tallahassee. Within days, Jonathan Robinson and Sherod McCall, planters from nearby Gadsden County, arrived with their slaves and constructed three crude log cabins for use by the territorial council. With the arrival of council members in November, Tallahassee began to function as the capital.

The cabins were not well suited to the council's needs nor did they project much in the way of the authority of the territorial government. Council members soon directed that a new, more substantial building be built to replace the cabins. In 1826 a two-story building, 40 by 26 feet, and constructed of brick and mortar, was completed. Although plans called for the quick expansion of this structure, budgetary problems halted construction. The existing building proved too small for the offices of the council and various other offices and, on March 3, 1839, the council approved $20,000, obtained through a congressional appropriation, for the design and construction of a larger, more commodious building.

The 1824 capitol was demolished and work started on a new building. Within a short time, construction slowed. The legislative council, faced with continuing monetary problems, appealed to the U.S. Congress for additional funds. Congress was not enthusiastic about the request and work on the capitol came to a standstill.

On May 25, 1843, Tallahassee, which at that time was principally a city of small wooden houses and stores, suffered a devastating fire. The blaze destroyed virtually all the businesses in the town and inflicted an estimated $500,000 in losses, and the city government passed an ordinance that mandated only "fireproof" buildings could be erected to replace those lost in the fire. As a result, the neighborhoods surrounding the partially completed capitol changed completely, becoming a section filled with "well arranged and commodious fire proof brick buildings." The blaze, according to one historian, marked the end of Tallahassee as a frontier village and its beginning as a true Southern capital.

Finally, Congress granted an additional $20,000 in 1844 and work resumed. The building was completed in 1845 in time for Florida's entry into the Union as a state and the inauguration of William D. Moseley on June 25. The construction of a grand and impressive capitol building in Tallahassee was a high water mark in the almost two decades of construction of public buildings throughout the plantation belt. New churches, schools, and meeting halls were built in towns throughout the region. Public buildings not only served specific purposes for their supporters, but such splendid structures with little to no commercial value became an unstated, yet highly visible symbol of the tremendous wealth of Florida's planters and their urban allies.

Few antebellum county government buildings survive today. Most were simply one- or two-room frame buildings, used primarily as courthouses. Many were in isolated rural areas, located conveniently between large plantations or farms, and frequently also served as meeting halls for political parties, social or fraternal groups, and churches.

As Florida moved from frontier territory to statehood, public buildings mirrored the citizens' fortunes, particularly the wealthy planters and their perceptions of their own importance. In just 40 years the northern part of the peninsula had gone from a sleepy colonial backwater to a prosperous and progressive Southern state. As Florida fell solidly under the influence of planters, its public architecture reflected their tastes and ambitions.

Tallahassee, which as late as 1840 was described as "a sleepy, unkempt and dirty little village," began to take on the appearance of a true urban area by the end of the decade. The log buildings, used for virtually all purposes—commercial, governmental, and residential—were replaced by stone, sawn lumber, and brick buildings after the disastrous fire of 1843. Despite periodic outbreaks of yellow fever, political turmoil, and occasional economic setbacks, the city moved slowly to achieve the appearance of other Southern capitals. In the small towns of North Florida similar changes took place, while in the old towns of Pensacola and St. Augustine, European-style architecture gave way to the more open and monumental styles of planter society.

The influence of plantation society continued to be felt in the architecture of public buildings until the 1880s when Victorian designs began to dominate. Today, Florida is home to virtually every style of building found on every continent in the world. But, for a large part of the 19th century, the style of public buildings remained firmly in the camp of Southern planters.

The construction of a modern capitol building, made of stone and masonry, marked the end of Florida as a territory and its beginning as a state. The new capitol ushered in a new period of public architecture and signaled the beginning of the end of Florida as a frontier. Gov. William D. Moseley, a planter who owned three plantations in Leon and Jefferson Counties, ensured that the interests of planters would be well served by state government. (Alma Clyde Field Library.)

The oldest original courthouse in Florida is in Manatee County, well south of the major plantation counties in North Florida, but in an area that had been selected for sugarcane plantations by Robert H. Gamble and Joseph Braden. Built in 1859– 1860 by Ezekiel Glazer, the courthouse served until the county seat was relocated in 1866. The building was then used as a Methodist church and Methodist parsonage before finally being relocated to the Manatee Village Historical Park. The Manatee Courthouse was restored in 1975.

The stark simplicity of the Manatee County Courthouse was decidedly different from the elaborate courthouse erected in 1835 in Jefferson County. A two-story building with a broad upstairs portico reached by a wide staircase with eighteen steps, a cupola graced the hip roof. Paid for by public subscription, the courthouse was remodeled several times to meet the demands of a growing population before it was replaced with a new building in 1909. One of the leading figures in the subscription movement was Abram Bellamy, who owned the large Nakoosa plantation a few miles from town.

In 1830 Benjamin Chaires, one the wealthiest planters in Leon County, constructed a small but solid building in the classical Greco-Roman style to house the first major bank in Florida. Located in the immediate vicinity of the planter's town home, The Columns, the bank became the center of a major political and economic battle during the late 1830s as Andrew Jackson's war on the National Bank was transposed to Florida. Created solely to provide credit and assistance to planters, the Union Bank experienced great difficulties in the Panic of 1837, with unsound banking practices and the upheavals of the Second Seminole Indian War. In 1843 it closed its doors. Nevertheless, the Union Bank building was quickly used for other purposes, including use as a Freedman's Bank during Reconstruction.

With the American annexation of Florida, private education institutions were introduced. Just 11 years after the ratification of the Adams-Onis Treaty, the citizens of Quincy, the town seat of Gadsden County, incorporated the Quincy Academy. Following the destruction of the original academy building by fire in 1849, leading citizens subscribed to a campaign to build a new facility. By 1851, the Quincy Academy was back in operation in a new building and offered a full curriculum of history, geology, geography, arithmetic, grammar, natural and moral philosophy, botany, and chemistry.

Although some legislators had engaged in debates about free public schools during the early 1850s, the costs of maintaining a system of public instruction was deemed to be too burdensome and the debates came to naught. The city government of Tallahassee, however, embraced the idea of free schools and by 1856 allocated a quarter of its annual budget of $8,500 to pay teachers' salaries. In 1855 the city also erected a stately Greco-Roman building to house the school. Tallahassee's experiment in public education was short lived, however, and by 1857, the city approached the state government with an offer to turn the academy building and some tax monies over to the State if the Seminary West of the Suwannee, a state-supported school, would be transferred there. The State agreed and the seminary, which eventually became Florida State University, opened its doors on October 1, 1857.

As Americans moved into Florida they created branches of institutions they had become familiar with in their home states. One of the earliest social organizations to gain a foothold in Florida was the Masons. The Grand Lodge of the Free and Accepted Masons of Georgia granted a charter to three separate lodges in Florida. Marianna received a charter for Harmony Lodge Number Three in 1829. Masonic Temples were built in each of these towns, but the most striking example of the antebellum buildings is found in the town of Quincy. Although the original temple was constructed in 1832, a cyclonic storm hit the town in 1851 and destroyed the hall. A decision was made to replace the destroyed building and, in 1852, work began on a new brick structure. The building was completed in 1854 and was utilized by the Washington Lodge until 1922 when the lodge moved into a new building. The 1850s structure is still in use today and serves as the home of the Quincy Woman's Club.

Churches were among the first public structures erected in antebellum Florida. One of the best examples of rural church construction is Moss Hill Methodist Church in Washington County. Built by planters using slave labor in 1857, Moss Hill Church represents the best example of classic architecture adapted to a frontier environment, using local materials. Moss Hill Church is still in occasional use today.

Left: The simple interior of Moss Hill Church was typical of small country churches in the rural areas of the plantation region. Such churches frequently became the setting for "hell fire and brimstone" sermons preached by itinerant evangelists who moved from church to church conducting revivals. Planters and their families often shared the same sanctuary as their slaves, and slaves often constituted the most faithful members of the congregation.

Below: Philadelphia Presbyterian Church, located outside Quincy, is another example of rural church architecture. Constructed in 1859 to replace an earlier 1828 log structure, Philadelphia Church was home to wealthy tobacco planters in Gadsden County. Severe in design, without even a steeple or portico, the church reflects the conservative values held by early Presbyterians in Florida. Compared to the ornate façade of the Cathedral in St. Augustine, Philadelphia Church and Moss Hill Church are models of simplicity.

Many small, rural churches served different denominations—a custom that continues today in the rural South—and to different classes of parishioners. In addition to providing religious succor, churches were important institutions for social activities, often played the role of community meeting house, and sometimes served as the focal point for political activities. Pisgah Methodist Church at Centreville in Leon County, for example, included a large number of yeoman farm families. Although planters generally controlled Florida politics, some issues, such as the bank question of the 1830s, riled the yeoman class and their opposition to such questions was often organized around congregational affiliations. One historian has remarked that such rural churches played an even more important role in civilizing the frontier, bringing a modicum of stability and civility to a rough-and-tumble society that often featured fighting, duels, and murder.

Pisgah Methodist Church, below, was also the spiritual home to some prominent planters, mostly transplants from Virginia. The early membership of this church included Francis Eppes, a grandson of Thomas Jefferson, and Thomas Eston Randolph, his father-in-law. The church was a simple white frame building with classic, but simple, lines. A contemporary remarked, "the simple outside of the Church masked the power of the parishioners inside."

Although it would never equal Tallahassee in importance, Pensacola was home to several wealthy factors and merchants. In 1830 Episcopalians in the city decided that the time had arrived for the construction of a church that was in keeping with their importance in town life. By 1832, members of the congregation held their first service in the new Christ Church, shown below. The substantial brick building still stands today.

Churches in small towns were somewhat more complex in their design. Middleburg is home to the Methodist Episcopal Church built in 1847. Middleburg, a small town in Clay County south of present-day Jacksonville, was a small transportation hub that linked St. Augustine to the St. Johns River. Several cotton and tobacco planters in the area used the town as an entrepot for their crops and for supplies for their plantations. Slaves owned by local planter George Branning supplied the labor necessary to erect the Gothic-styled structure and its center steeple out of heart pine and hand-wrought nails.

Apalachicola, one of the busiest of Florida's cotton, timber, and tobacco ports, was a flourishing port town during the antebellum period. Wealthy merchants who handled the shipments of unfinished agricultural products from Georgia, Alabama, and North Florida and the reverse shipments of finished goods upriver spent a great deal of money on fine homes and public buildings. In 1837 the Episcopal congregation decided to erect a building that was indicative of their status as well-to-do merchants, would recognize the overall wealth of the community, and would proclaim the strength of their beliefs to a secular world. The result, Trinity Episcopal Church was designed and built of white pine in New York. Shipped by schooner around the tip of the Florida peninsula to Apalachicola, the church was reassembled with wooden pins. Trinity Episcopal Church is still active today.

The First Presbyterian Church in Tallahassee, built in 1838, was also designed to capture the growing importance of the capital city in Florida life and the inordinate wealth of its planter parishioners. The original cost of $13,370.60 was largely borne by the sale of pews, which generated $12,500.00. Solidly built of local bricks and timber, First Presbyterian Church is one of the few territorial period buildings still standing in Tallahassee. The interface between First Presbyterian's planter families and the state government was immediate and continues today. In 1826 Rev. Henry White became the first of several ministers from the church to serve as chaplain to the Florida legislature, which was under the control of planters throughout the antebellum period. The First Presbyterian Church anchored a collection of several churches in the immediate vicinity. Standing nearby were the Methodist Episcopal Church, the Protestant Methodist Church, and St. Johns Episcopal Church. In 1846 a Catholic church was added to the mix. Today, First Presbyterian Church, with its tall spire and stately Doric columns, continues to occupy a prominent place in the city's skyline.

In Jacksonville, the small port city at the mouth of the St. Johns, worshippers attended the stately but small St. Paul's Methodist Church. St. Paul's served its congregation throughout the Civil War and until 1890, when the Catholic Church purchased the building. In 1901 St. Paul's was destroyed in the fire that decimated most of the city's downtown.

Not all public buildings in antebellum Florida were built by individuals, church congregations, or state or county governments. In 1832 Congress passed an act that authorized the construction of an arsenal in Gadsden County. Originally named Mt. Vernon, the arsenal was made up of four brick buildings to form a quadrangle of some four acres. The arsenal served as an arms storage depot during the Second Seminole War, as a staging encampment for Florida troops in the Civil War, as a Freedman's Bureau headquarters in Reconstruction, as a penitentiary in the late 1860s, and finally as a state mental hospital in the late 1800s and the 1900s. As the result of its varied uses over time, the arsenal never achieved a distinctive architectural style. Today, only the magazine and officer's quarters remain from the original buildings. The immense size of the arsenal and its brick and wood fascia was appropriately imposing to satisfy the pretensions of Florida's emerging planter society.

Above: An early artist's rendering shows the U. S. Arsenal at Chattahoochee. This facility was a major source of arms for Florida's soldiers in 1861 and also served as the place where Florida troops were inducted into Confederate service.

Right: By October 1856, the Pensacola & Georgia Railroad was transporting sightseers and cotton bales from the Tallahassee area, and, by January 1858, the P&G had opened a connection with Jefferson County at Bailey's Mill.

In June 1860 David Levy Yulee's railroad reached the Gulf Shore and was recognized as the first railroad to do so. The Florida Railroad tapped the rapidly developing cotton plantations in Marion and Alachua Counties. It also carried passengers who wanted to shorten their journey to California and could now cross the peninsula to make connections with ships at Cedar Key, thereby eliminating the need to sail south around the Florida Keys. Among the first public buildings to be constructed was the Island Hotel, which provided lodging for ship's captains, tradesmen, and passengers. Cedar Key's importance was curtailed after only a few months. In April 1861 Florida, now a Confederate state, was at war. Among the first actions taken by the Union was to capture Cedar Key and its railhead. For a brief period after the war, Cedar Key enjoyed a return to prosperity when it was the main shipping port for cedar logs gathered in the surrounding swamps. Today, it is a small, sleepy fishing village periodically overwhelmed by tourists.

Chapter Four

HOMES OF FLORIDA'S PLANTER ARISTOCRACY
Leon County

Given the limited size of Florida's plantation region, some planters chose to build their primary residences in towns that were very close by. Many of the state's largest plantations were located within a few miles of the capital and owners kept a watchful eye on what went on in the city. Some planters maintained secondary residences in the city, while others built their primary residence there and used their country houses only sparingly. Indeed, many of the once remote plantations in modern-day Leon County were only a few miles from the center of Tallahassee, and today's urban sprawl has surrounded them or simply built over the sites of these once magnificent mansions. Yet, despite the inexorable push of modern society, some of these great houses still remain and still exude the confidence and certainty of wealth and privilege their original owners possessed.

Since few permanent building materials like stone were readily at hand, plantation structures were usually made of wood that was sawn from the vast supply of native pines and hardwoods covering the region. Even as the plantation society matured and planters made their fortunes, wood remained the building material of choice, although a few of the wealthiest planters made use of bricks and stone. Slave craftsmen were experts in the use of wood, and their creations rivaled those in the older established areas of the South.

Leon County was home to some 90 or so large plantations at various times and, as the center of planter power, possessed some of the most pretentious residences. In 1850 the census listed 81 plantation owners in the county, several with two or more plantations in their possession. Few of the original plantation homes in Leon County have survived until today, but in the immediate Civil War era, names like Whitehall, Buena Vista, Clairveau, Iamonia, and Betton Hall were familiar to county residents. Some have been destroyed to make way for urban development, while still more have suffered the indignity of neglect and inevitable collapse.

Although Leon County planters enjoyed the prestige of residing near the state capital, the surrounding counties of Jefferson, Madison, Jackson, and Gadsden and were home to a significant number of planters whose wealth and estates equaled or exceeded theirs. Most of the planters of these four counties had close family, political, and economic ties with the planters in Leon.

Above: An artist sketched this rendering of Verdura, the plantation home of Benjamin Chaires in Leon County.

Left: Perhaps none of the achievements of Florida planters exceeded those of Benjamin Chaires of Leon County. A native of North Carolina, Chaires, along with his two brothers, arrived in Tallahassee by way of Milledgeville, the capital of Georgia, and Jacksonville, where he was credited with devising the plan for the city's growth. A man of many interests, he was involved in banking, railroad, shipping, and construction. Once acknowledged as the wealthiest planter in Florida, Chaires owned a plantation of more than 9,000 acres just a few miles east of Tallahassee, where he built one of the greatest and most beautiful plantation homes, Verdura, a 13-room brick house that rose three stories into the Florida sky. Although Verdura was consumed by fire in 1885, several soot-stained columns still mark the site today. (Florida State Archives.)

This was not the only plantation Chaires owned, nor was Verdura his only residence. At various times during the antebellum period, he was the owner of Bolton, a large plantation located on the Old St. Augustine Road southeast of Tallahassee. In addition to his rural residences, Chaires also owned The Columns, long regarded as the finest antebellum residence in Tallahassee. Located at the prestigious corner of Adams Street and Park Avenue, this stately house, characterized by its four columns and dark-red brick outer walls, was considered to be part of the city's "architectural" triangle that also included the capitol and The Grove. Thus, Chaires was the owner of the two "most beautiful" houses in pre-Civil war Florida.

The holdings of Benjamin Chaires were so extensive that when they were divided after his death, his children—Martha, Charles, and Thomas—were still among the largest planters in Leon County.

Richard Keith Call, a protégé of Andrew Jackson and twice a territorial governor (1835–1840; 1841–1844), settled just east of the state capitol on the edge of Tallahassee. Although primarily a politician, Call was a speculator in land, a railroad investor, and, above all, a planter. His home, The Grove, was located on the very edge of Tallahassee and embodied the best of classical plantation architecture, including a large pediment supported by four tall columns. Construction on the house started in 1825 and probably was completed in 1829.

While Call's political activities required him to stay close to the capital, the 1840 Census listed his wealth at some 6,000 acres of prime land, 66 slaves, and numerous lots in Tallahassee—and his ties to the planter elite of Florida were substantial. The Grove was his principal residence, but Call also owned several more plantations, including Orchard Pond, located on the shores of Lake Jackson. At one time, he was both the largest landowner and largest slaveholder in Leon County. It was only fitting then that his town residence reflected his wealth and the values of the planting class.

There were other reasons for Call to build such a distinguished home, and The Grove has a romantic history to it as well. According to family legend, Richard K. Call married Mary Kirkman of Tennessee in a lavish ceremony at Gen. Andrew Jackson's home, The Hermitage, near Nashville. Although Call was a favorite of the general's, the Kirkman family was politically opposed to Jackson and felt that Mary's marriage to his protégé was wrong. Since the new bride had broken with her family to marry the man she loved, the bridegroom supposedly was moved to build her a large and opulent home in Florida to replace the large house she had given up to marry him.

The Grove has had a long association with Florida politics, particularly the Democrat Party, and served as the official mansion of the governor during the term of LeRoy Collins in the 1960s. Today, Mary Call Collins, a descendant of Richard Keith Call and the widow of Governor Collins, maintains the home on a spacious estate immediately across the street from Florida's newest governor's mansion.

One of the richest and most influential families in antebellum Florida was the Croom family. Originally from Lenoir County, North Carolina, the four Croom brothers liquidated their family holdings in the Tarheel state and moved to Florida in the early 1830s. One brother, George Alexander Croom, owned a large plantation in Gadsden County, while a second brother, Richard, owned Oakland, located near Tallahassee on Miccosukee Road. A third brother, Hardy Bryan Croom, owned one plantation near present-day Marianna and another near Quincy. In 1836 Hardy Croom and the fourth brother, Bryan, the best known of all the Croom brothers, purchased four sections of prime farm land on Lake Lafayette near Tallahassee. In 1837 Hardy Croom, along with his entire family, perished aboard the steamboat *Home* off Cape Hatteras.

Bryan Croom, whose 195 slaves and $105,000 in real estate made him one of the four largest planters in Leon County in 1850, was the proud owner of Goodwood, the largest and most beautiful of the surviving antebellum homes in Leon County. Designed by architect George Anderson and completed in 1839, this Georgian structure was surrounded by formal English gardens, a private racetrack, winding carriage drives, bridle paths, and seven guest cottages. Three stables surrounded a large carriage house. The home featured the very latest in residential appliances and furnishings, and family and guests were fed from a kitchen located northwest of the mansion.

In addition to his plantations in Leon, Jefferson, and Gadsden Counties, Bryan Croom, like other wealthy planters, invested in a number of enterprises. Despite his great wealth and prestige, Croom was brought down by a troublesome lawsuit that spanned a full 20 years in various courts.

When Hardy Croom and his entire family died in the *Home* sinking, his mother-in-law, Henrietta Smith, and his sister-in-law, Elizabeth Armistead, brought suit to claim his estate. The case focused on the question of presumption of survival—that is, the question of which member of the family was the last to drown—and whether the laws of North Carolina or Florida would govern the inheritance.

Although he owned considerable property in Florida and had sold his North Carolina holdings, Hardy Croom had nevertheless maintained his legal residence in that state. Bryan Croom, having purchased any interest in the estate that might accrue to his other relatives, maintained his brother had boarded the *Home* with his family with the explicit purpose of making Florida his permanent home. As a result, argued lawyers for Bryan Croom, the entire estate should belong to him. Although his claim was initially upheld in Circuit Court, in 1857 the Florida Supreme Court overturned the ruling on an appeal filed by Smith and Armistead. As a result, Bryan Croom was forced to liquidate his holdings and soon left Florida.

Ownership of Goodwood passed to Henrietta Smith, who sold it to Arvah Hopkins. Since then, the plantation has been owned by Dr. William Lamb Arrowsmith, an Englishman of "great mystery;" Mrs. Fanny Tiers, reputedly the wealthiest woman in the world; and W.C. Hodges, who bought it in 1925. When Hodges died in 1940, ownership passed to his wife, Margaret. In 1948 Margaret Wilson Hodges married Thomas M. Hood. Soon after Margaret's death in 1978, Thomas Hood established the Margaret E. Wilson Foundation to oversee the restoration and operation of Goodwood. With his death in 1990, the foundation assumed control of the property and operates it today as the Goodwood Museum and Gardens.

Above: Bellevue was moved to a new location in order to preserve it. Originally located on a 560-acre plantation owned by Richard Hayward, Bellevue became the home of Catherine Murat in the 1850s.

The widow of Prince Achille Murat, nephew of the Emperor Napoleon I of France and son of the former King of Naples, was the daughter of Boyd Willis, a Virginian planter who had settled near Tallahassee. Catherine had a distinguished pedigree of her own—she was the great-grandniece of Georgia Washington—and became the doyen of planter social life in Jefferson County. Lipona, the Murat plantation on the Wacissa River, was the favorite place for planter families to visit, and the story circulated that the Murats had converted their home's second floor into small bedrooms to accommodate their guests. The Murats owned a second plantation, Econchatti, but nothing is known about that property.

Catherine continued to hold court at Lipona after Prince Murat died in 1847. Napoleon III assumed the French throne in 1852 and offered Catherine a chalet in France. She refused the offer, preferring to remain among her friends in Florida. She nevertheless experienced a considerable influence in her fortunes as the new emperor moved to restore the properties of the Napoleonic nobility. In the 1850s Catherine Murat moved from Lipona to Bellevue. From there she created a lively circle friends and admirers and entertained until well after the Civil War.

In 1967 Bellevue was moved from its original site on Jackson Bluff Road to a site adjoining the Tallahassee Junior Museum. It is open to the public. (Painting by Claribel B. Jett, Tallahassee Junior Museum.)

Chapter Five
HOMES OF FLORIDA'S PLANTER ARISTOCRACY
Jefferson and Madison Counties

Perhaps the most famous Jefferson County plantation was El Destino, originally developed by William B. Nutthall, who had moved to Florida from Virginia. El Destino's fame rests more on the 1927 publication of the extensive records of the plantation, after it was sold to George Noble Jones of Savannah, Georgia. Jones, owner of Wormsloe outside of Savannah, also purchased another 1,600-acre Leon County plantation, Chemonie. Although he continued to maintain his residence in Georgia, Jones required the overseers to report every aspect of the management of both plantations on a bi-weekly basis, and these reports and the plantation journals detailed the daily life of overseers, slaves, and tradesmen on the farm. These journals became the basis for Florida Plantation Records from the Papers of George Noble Jones by Ulrich B. Phillips and James D. Glunt. Additional records are housed in the Alma Clyde Field Library of Florida History in Cocoa, Florida.

Like the planters in Leon County, those in Jefferson County also played an important role in the political, social, and economic activities of the antebellum period. As men or the sons of men who had carved a plantation society out of the frontier of Florida, they felt entitled to rule despite the fact that

the 1850 Census listed only some 45 planters in a population of 2,775 whites and 377 farms. At the heart of their power and prestige was the ownership of more than 5,500 slaves and the fact that they produced 74 percent of the county's 9,468 bales of cotton.

Madison County was preferred as an area of settlement by many South Carolina transplants to Florida, and their affinity for the "red hills" of Madison was also shared by a number of expatriates from Georgia. Two-thirds of the county's 33 large planters in 1850 were from the Palmetto State and, like their brethren in other plantation counties, accounted for the majority (73 percent) of the 5,024 bales of cotton produced in 1850. Unlike other plantation counties, Madison had a white majority population (2,802 whites and 2,688 slaves) and was the state's leader in butter and cheese production.

None of Madison County's antebellum plantation houses have survived to the present. Conversations with local historians indicate that those that survived the Civil War were allowed to fall into ruin and were eventually torn down. Yet, Madison County's planters played an important role in antebellum Florida's economic, social, and political scene.

Casa Bianca was the home of Joseph M. White and his wife Ellen, whose nickname was "Florida," and was the center of a 3,000-acre cotton plantation. White was the leader of the anti-Jackson political movement in Florida and spent 12 years as the state's delegate to Congress during the territorial period. A native of Kentucky and a skilled lawyer, White first settled in Pensacola where his fluency in French and Spanish, plus his very cosmopolitan demeanor, formed the basis of his considerable success.

Casa Bianca, a massive three-story frame mansion, served as an appropriate backdrop for White's wife, who was reputed to be the most beautiful woman in the world. Vivacious and socially polished, Ellen White was a favorite of Washington society and, on several European tours, hobnobbed with the rich and powerful in England and the continent. When Joseph White died in 1839, Ellen retained ownership of Casa Bianca, although she spent little time at the plantation.

Kidder M. Moore, who owned the Planter's Hotel in Tallahassee, sold his business and moved to Jefferson County to try his luck at planting. In 1847 he was in residence at Lipona, but he soon moved to Pine Tucky. That year Moore suffered a devastating loss when four of his slaves—all prime field hands—ran away. He offered a $300.00 reward for their return, along with a female and an older male who had run away previously. The main house at Pine Tucky was a two-story structure, simple in design, which overlooked the flatwoods leading to the Gulf.

Near Casa Bianca was Abram Bellamy's Nakoosa, a plantation that extended for more than four miles. Bellamy, a captain in the Florida militia during the Second Seminole War, was an influential planter and served several terms on the territorial council. He was one of the original founders of the Democratic Party in Florida, one of the delegates who authored the St. Joseph constitution in 1838, and a leading proponent of statehood. On the local scene, he was one of the trustees of the local academy, on the committee that approved the construction of a county courthouse in 1839, and a strong proponent of the creation of a state university in Jefferson County—a project that never reached fruition.

Another early Jefferson County settler from South Carolina was Martin Palmer, a native of Edgefield. With his wife and nine children (plus slaves), Palmer arrived in Florida in 1829 and chose land near Monticello for his plantation. In addition to his planting activities, he owned and operated a general store and a tavern. Palmer also was one of the founding subscribers to the Southern Rights Manufacturing Association, which built and operated a cotton mill in Monticello. This project, which sprang out of the Nashville Convention in 1850, was tied to the idea that the South and the institution of slavery were in grave danger. Southerners were urged to become self-sufficient and to stop relying on the North for anything.

Throughout the South, southern nationalists began to sponsor the creation of mills, foundries, and other industries that would lessen the dependency of the region on external sources for its economic survival. Martin Palmer died in 1857, just three years before Florida seceded, but he passed his strong sense of southern nationalism to his sons. One son, Thomas Martin Palmer, was a delegate to the state's Secession Convention and later served as a surgeon with the 2nd Florida Regiment. Palmer's other sons who were of age also served in the Confederate military. The Palmer family retained the estate until the 1880s.

Still another South Carolinian who settled in Jefferson County during the 1830s was Burwell McBride, whose Rosewood plantation was south of Dolce Domum and adjacent to Robert Gamble's Welaunee plantation of some 6,300 acres. McBride died in 1848, and ownership of Rosewood passed to his daughter, Catherine G. Cole, the widow of Richard B. Cole. Catherine managed the plantation until her death in 1855, when the plantation became the property of her son-in-law, Asa May, and his wife, Margaret, a granddaughter of Burwell McBride. In addition to Rosewood, a modest but beautiful home, May owned several other properties throughout the county.

Not only was May a successful planter, but like other neighbors, he was involved in a variety of business enterprises. In 1851 he was a director of the Wacissa and Aucilla Navigation Company, which proposed to dig a canal to link the Wacissa River with the St. Marks River as a means of expediting the transport of cotton and tobacco to St. Marks, a port on the Gulf of Mexico. Although this project was never completed, it was one of several transportation efforts—roads, railroads, and canals—supported with varying degrees of success by Florida planters. When the Civil War came, May supported the Confederacy and, in 1861, was a district representative on a statewide committee to provide relief to the families of soldiers in the military. In 1865 he served as a delegate to the state's constitutional convention charged with writing into law the mandates of President Andrew Johnson's unsuccessful program of presidential Reconstruction. In 1876 May served as a member of the Jefferson County Board of Commissioners. May died in 1881, and the executors of his estate sold his holdings at a public auction. Today Rosewood has been restored to its original condition and is open to the public on a restricted basis.

William J. Bailey, a veteran of the Second Seminole War, also owned a plantation of considerable size in Jefferson County. Lyndhurst was soon the focal point of society, and the two-story mansion, set among stately oak trees, hosted all of the leading social, literary, and political lights of antebellum Florida. William J. Bailey died in 1872, and his family continued to occupy Lyndhurst until 1964, when the mansion was sold. Lyndhurst still functions as a plantation today, although its 3,500 acres are given over to cattle ranching and farming.

In 1835 Dr. Theodore Turnbull, a recent graduate of the Charleston Medical School, arrived to establish a practice in Monticello and Jefferson County. Although he maintained his practice in town, Turnbull lived on a plantation, Sunrise, which he apparently rented until his death in 1845. A popular figure in local society, Turnbull was also involved in a movement to disavow the effort by the tax collector to collect property taxes in "specie" only following the suspension of payments by the Union Bank in 1837. During the 1830s, the question of banks and government support proved disruptive in Florida politics. Friendship and kinship frequently were forgotten as prominent planters took opposing views on the question.

In 1856 his son, Theodore Turnbull Jr., purchased the property, and the plantation remained in family hands until 1913.

Reddin W. Parramore, a Georgian from Telfair County, owned a large cotton plantation but concentrated on raising cattle. Parramore was the owner of five different plantations in the county, and when he died in 1851, he left a personal estate valued at $89,600. Although he owned a tremendous number of acres in farmland, Parramore preferred to live in Madison, one-third of which was co-owned by Parramore and his brother-in-law Simeon Alexander of Thomas County, Georgia. His home, made of hand-hewn boards, wooden pegs, and handmade square nails, was built in 1839 and is still standing on North Range Street in the city.

While Parramore might have preferred town living, other Madison County planters built large houses on their plantations. (Photo by Betty Oliver and Robert Fischer.)

Richard J. Mays, a native of South Carolina, was the proud owner of Clifton, while his brother, Dr. Rhydon C. Mays, owned 1,800 acres of prime land. Rhydon C. Mays sold his interests in Madison County in 1852 and moved to Putnam County on the St. Johns River to grow oranges.

Chapter Six

HOMES OF FLORIDA'S PLANTER ARISTOCRACY
Gadsden and Jackson Counties

Although Jefferson, Leon, and Madison Counties constituted the heart of the antebellum cotton belt in Florida, Gadsden and Jackson Counties were also important elements in creating an "Old South" society in the state. Most of the Jackson County planters, many of whom came from North Carolina, were located in the central portion of the county, along the Chipola River, or along a line between Marianna and Campbellton. Although a few of the early settlers had concentrated on the production of sugarcane, by the 1840s virtually all of them concentrated on the production of cotton, while a few joined their neighbors in adjoining Gadsden County and made tobacco their principal crop.

Jackson County, unlike other plantation counties, was the scene of a major invasion by the federal army during the Civil War. The county seat of Marianna was defended by a hodgepodge of troops—mostly old men, convalescents, and young boys—but fell to Union forces under the command of Gen. Alexander Asboth in September 1864. Although federal forces soon retreated, they took with them several hundred slaves, timber, and other critical supplies. Asboth made no effort to drive his forces the small distance to Tallahassee, and that city remained the sole Confederate capital east of

the Mississippi River to escape capture and occupation by Union troops during the war.

John Milton, the pro-secession Civil War governor of Florida, owned Sylvania, the 2,800-acre plantation that served as his principal residence. By 1860, however, he had managed to acquire more than 7,000 acres. In addition to his duties as a planter, Milton practiced law, was a major general in the Florida militia, and served as a member of the state's house of representatives. As governor, he, unlike some of his contemporaries, fully supported the Confederate government. When the end came in 1865, Milton addressed the legislature one last time and declared "death was preferable to living in the Union." Following his address, he left Tallahassee for Sylvania, where, according to popular history, he immediately went upstairs to his bedroom, placed his shotgun under his chin, and pulled the trigger. Milton never lived to see the Union flag fly again over the state capitol.

Not every farmer owned slaves or considered himself a planter in antebellum Jackson County. The number of small farms owned by yeoman farmers grew from 287 in 1850 to 581 in 1860. During the same decade, the county's racial balance moved from being a majority of African Americans to having a majority of whites. Yeoman farmers also engaged in the production of cash crops like cotton and tobacco, and in 1860 yeoman farmers on farms of 100 to 500 acres produced 41 percent of the county's crop of 8,635 bales.

Gadsden County, which lies between Jackson and Jefferson Counties, was also considered prime cotton country, although a number of its planters chose to concentrate their major efforts toward the cultivation of tobacco. Many of the largest planters in Gadsden County had close family connections with planters in the surrounding counties, and with the exception of a few European immigrants, most hailed from North Carolina, South Carolina, or Virginia.

Gadsden County was home to a number of large planters during the antebellum period. The diversification of crops—tobacco and cotton—ensured that the county's planters and yeoman farmers profited during these years, perhaps to a greater extent than their neighbors in adjacent counties. Like its

neighbors to the east, Gadsden County suffered little in the way of raids or military excursions during the Civil War, and many of its plantations survived intact. Planters, who had grown rich on the labor of slaves, found themselves trying to preserve their fortunes and lands in the postwar years with free labor. In the face of competition from new sources of cotton and tobacco that emerged during the Union blockade of the South, this task became more and more difficult as the years went by.

Large plantations frequently were subdivided into small tenant farms or sharecropper acreage and the efficiencies of a single agricultural operation gave way to the inefficiencies of multiple operations of subsistence farmers. Gradually, the larger land holdings were sold off and, although a few specialized plantations remain today, they passed from the scene. Nevertheless, the legacy of the Middle Florida planters is how they shaped Florida's history during the first 45 years of the state's history.

Francis R. Ely moved to Marianna from Plymouth, North Carolina, in 1839. According to the tax records of Jackson County, by 1845 he had acquired a plantation of 1,629 acres and a labor force of 63 slaves.

Ely erected a residence suitable to a man of his stature on the outskirts of Marianna and near the intersection of the Campbellton and St. Andrews Roads. A corner of his land was used as the primary fortification against federal troops attacking Marianna, but the Ely homestead escaped major damage.

Although Francis R. Ely died in 1858, the home remained in family hands until 1888, when it was sold to W.J. Daniel, a Marianna banker. It was subsequently owned by Francis B. Carter, a Florida Supreme Court justice, and by Mrs. Joseph M. Criglar.

The home of Hamilton Bryan, Great Oaks is one of the few antebellum plantation homes that remain today in Jackson County. The house was constructed in 1857, and unlike some of its stately neighbors, it managed to escape major damage during the war.

Almost lost to the ravages of time and the elements, Great Oaks still survives today as one of the foremost examples of Jackson County plantation architecture.

Now fully restored to its antebellum glory, Hamilton Bryan's Great Oaks is a major attraction for visitors to the Florida Panhandle.

Small farmers such as John A. Syfrett, who purchased 150 acres in 1839 in the small, rural village of Greenwood, were important cogs in the agricultural machinery of Jackson County. Some evidence exists indicating that the Syfrett family may have "squatted" on the land as early as 1837. Although the Syfretts were not among the landed gentry of Jackson County, they were well-respected farmers, and their home, though modest compared to some of the surrounding plantation homes, was surrounded by outbuildings that indicated their solid middle-class status. A barn, smoke house, carriage house, office building, and a small slave cabin give mute testimony that the Syfrett family had prospered in Jackson County. The Syfrett farm was sold to Mary Roberts in 1851 and the title later passed through the hands of Henry Bryan to Dr. Franklin Hart in 1855. In 1861 the property was purchased by M.F. Erwin and has been in the Erwin family ever since.

The Syfrett homestead, now known as the Erwin House, has been fully restored and a second-story porch added to the front of the house. Obstructing trees and shrubs have been cleared to provide a much better view of the home as it might have looked in the 1850s.

Among the earliest planters to take up residence was Augustus H. Lanier, whose large plantation in Gadsden County was matched by another one in Madison County consisting of some 1,600 acres. Lanier concentrated on cotton production and was recognized as the second largest grower in the county in the 1840s and early 1850s. He was also the proud owner of one of the most beautiful and best-known manor houses in the area. His house, which was built in 1837, survived until the 1970s.

Another North Carolina transplant was Willoughby Shackelford Gregory, whose brother, Jason Gregory, had a fine plantation in Calhoun County. William Gregory came to Florida in 1824 and by 1850 had acquired some 700 acres and more than 30 slaves. Like his brother, Willoughby Gregory prospered as a cotton and tobacco planter.

By 1860, Willoughby Gregory had increased his land holdings to more than 2,000 acres. Around 1843, Gregory built a splendid home for his family. Unusual in its use of brick construction and its use of a continuous foundation instead of piers, the house was probably the handiwork of local mason Charles Waller, who was active in the construction of most of the large homes in Calhoun and surrounding counties.

The Gregory family moved between Calhoun and Gadsden Counties several times, but the Gadsden home remained most closely identified with the family.

The Willoughby Gregory home still survives today.

Jason Gregory Jr., a brother to Willoughby, owned a large plantation across the river near Ocheesee Landing. During the Civil War, a Confederate gun battery was located on the nearby bluffs to prevent Union gunboats from using the Apalachicola River as a thoroughfare into Alabama and Georgia.

Chapter Six

OUTSIDE MIDDLE FLORIDA
The East Coast and St. Johns River

Not all of Florida's plantations were located in the five counties of Middle Florida, and not all were tied directly to the planting aristocracy of North Carolina, Virginia, South Carolina, or Georgia. Twenty years of British control between 1763 and 1783 saw the transfer of the Caribbean and North American plantation models to the Florida peninsula. Although few in number, these plantations often developed on the foundations of earlier Spanish efforts to build viable hacienda units, but which often failed because of the unreliability of Native American laborers, the benign neglect of colonial authorities, and the allure of more profitable ventures in Central and South America. The ill-defined status of slaves and the institution of hereditary slavery in the Spanish legal system also contributed to the failure of large agricultural operations. Despite awarding large land grants to various individuals, only a few chose to invest the time, money, and energy necessary to develop large estates like those in Cuba or Mexico. Charlton W. Tebeau, whose *A History of Florida* is considered mandatory reading for every student of Florida history, summed up the impact of 250 years of Spanish ownership with this succinct, but accurate sentence, "The smallness of the Spanish achievement in Florida is difficult to realize." Although Spain received another chance to do more when it recovered the peninsula in 1763, its record was not any better the second time around.

The tenuous hold the British had on Florida did not promote a sense of permanency for the few English settlers who came to the region, nor did the Loyalists who came south to escape the wrath of their colonial neighbors during the American Revolution view Florida as much more than a temporary refuge until the war was over. Like the Spanish before them, British authorities did encourage colonization through generous land grants, but these efforts contributed little. Between 1764 and 1774, authorities in St. Augustine granted 1,440,000 acres to 114 persons in East Florida, but only 22 of the grants were actually settled. An additional 210,000 acres were given to 576 families in the area. In West Florida, authorities in Pensacola issued 45 grants for a total of 350,000 acres, but these grants remained unsettled.

While West Florida failed to attract new settlers, East Florida was home to approximately 100 plantations, the most successful of which belonged to Gov. James Grant and his successor, Patrick Tonyn, as well as to Lt. Gov. John Moultrie. Grant's plantation was located near St. Augustine and produced indigo, while Tonyn's operation was situated on the St. Johns River. Moultrie, whose Bella Vista plantation was on the Matanzas River, also developed Rosetta on the Tomoka River near present-day Daytona. Some 180 slaves provided the labor necessary to clear the land, plant rice crops in the marshes, and gather turpentine from some 25,000 trees.

Private individuals also enjoyed some limited success. Denys Rolle attempted to take advantage of the 80,000 acres granted to him by British authorities. Although he first attempted to use indentured laborers for his plantation near Palatka, this effort failed. Another attempt, this time with the use of inmates of debtor prisons, also failed. Finally, he enjoyed some success with slave labor; however, as an absentee owner, he could not stop his agent from stealing the profits of the plantation. His efforts to tame the Florida wilderness ended when the British departed in 1783.

Stretching from present-day Palm Coast to the southern tip of Volusia County, a string of 17 plantations provided opportunities for planters to wrestle considerable wealth from the Florida soil. The development of more plantations in the region was severely curtailed by the fierce fighting in the Second Seminole War, and the area never fully recovered from this conflict. The plantation region in Middle Florida also diverted many of the planters who might have shown interest in this region. Not much is known about some of the earliest plantations along Florida's eastern coast, but their names are still remembered, and historical markers dot the region marking their locations.

British governor James Grant followed a policy of issuing land grants to British citizens to colonize of Florida.

Above left: Gov. Patrick Tonyn was the owner of a plantation near the St. Johns River.

Above right: John Moultrie, who served as Florida's lieutenant governor under Grant, owned Bella Vista on the Matanzas River. He also developed a plantation named Rosetta on the Tomoka River.

In 1764 a wealthy and enterprising Scot named Richard Oswald received a land grant in present-day Volusia County where he established four separate plantations. He cut canals through the marshes of the Halifax River to support his indigo, rice, and sugarcane crops, but he ultimately lost his lands.

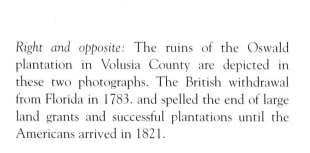

Right and opposite: The ruins of the Oswald plantation in Volusia County are depicted in these two photographs. The British withdrawal from Florida in 1783. and spelled the end of large land grants and successful plantations until the Americans arrived in 1821.

During the years from 1783 until 1821, Spain once again controlled Florida. Although the Spanish government made generous concessions to attract American settlers to Florida, few took advantage of these enticements. John McQueen, a veteran of the American Revolution from South Carolina, moved to Florida in the early 1790s. In 1793 he received Fort George Island from Spanish authorities and with his 300 slaves cleared land for a cotton plantation. McQueen built a substantial but simple plantation home in 1798. Within a few years, McQueen faced bankruptcy following a season of unusually high waters and a meager cotton crop. John Houston McIntosh of Georgia purchased the holdings of McQueen on the St. Johns River in 1803. Although McIntosh managed to restore the plantation to prosperity, his involvement in border politics ended his stay. McIntosh was one of the leaders of the abortive independence movement of 1812, known as the Patriot Rebellion, that led to the momentary creation of the "Territory of East Florida." Following the failure of the Patriots to gain recognition of their new government by President James Madison, the movement came to a dismal end. McIntosh, who had sworn allegiance to Spain when he became a Florida planter, realized that Spain would probably exact a harsh penalty from the rebels. He decided that his interests were best served by a return to Georgia.

Zephaniah Kingsley, who had first arrived in Florida in 1803 and who had a plantation, Laurel Grove, on the St. Johns River, leased McIntosh's now vacant plantation in 1814. Three years later, he purchased the property outright. Kingsley

Tabby slave cabin are shown in ruins.

resided on this plantation until 1837, when he moved his family to Haiti. Kingsley was an unusual individual. In addition to his planting activities, he was also a slave trader who dealt directly with suppliers in Africa. In 1806 he purchased a female slave, Anna Madgigine Jai, with whom he lived with as man and wife for 37 years and by whom he fathered five children. Spanish authorities informally tolerated interracial marriages, and Kingsley acknowledged Anna as his wife and, in 1811, granted her and his children by her their freedom. She managed his plantation on Fort George Island for 23 years. There she had her own house, bought and sold slaves, and performed the role of mistress of the property. In legal documents, Kingsley recognized Anna and her children as his legal heirs, although their rights to own property were subject to more restrictive

laws after the Americans took control of Florida in 1821. While the practice of cohabitating with slaves was not unknown in planter circles, his public recognition of Anna as his wife placed Kingsley outside the pale of white society.

As American ownership of Florida resulted in an ever-increasing growth in population, Kingsley's ability to live openly with Anna as his common-law wife was subject to greater scrutiny. In 1837 Kingsley moved Anna and their children to Haiti and, in 1839, sold his plantation to his nephews. Kingsley died in 1843, and Anna remained in Haiti until 1847, when she returned to Florida to live on a farm she had purchased. Anna Kingsley survived the upheavals of the Civil War and the abolition of slavery. She died in 1870 at the age of 77.

With the acquisition of Florida, Americans began to arrive in greater numbers. Although the richer cotton and tobacco lands of Middle Florida attracted the most settlers, a small number looked to settle in East Florida, particularly along the St. Johns River or the coast. One such settler was Maj. Charles W. Bulow of South Carolina, whose plantation, Bulowville, at the headwaters of the Halifax River was considered an ideal location for the cultivation of sugarcane and citrus. His son, Joachim, inherited the 4,675-acre plantation when Major Bulow died in 1823. A force of some 300 slaves cultivated about 1,000 acres of sugarcane, 1,200 acres of cotton, and other subsistence crops. In the early 1830s Bulow used his slaves to erect rather substantial stone buildings to house his sugar mill and other shops necessary to run the plantation. During the early days of the Second Seminole War, Maj. Benjamin A. Putnam used the plantation as his headquarters. Unfortunately, when Putnam lost the confrontation at Dunlawton plantation further south, the Bulow plantation was abandoned and immediately laid waste to by the Indians.

Dunlawton plantation was the home of Sarah Anderson and her two sons, George and James, who purchased a large tract of land from Mr. Lawton, a land dealer from Charleston, in 1832. Combining her maiden name, Dunn, with Lawton's name produced the plantation's unique title. Following the example of their fellow planters in the area, the Andersons concentrated on the production of sugarcane. They, too, constructed solid buildings of coquina stones and brick to house the expensive equipment it took to turn cane squeezings into sugar and molasses. Prosperous and thriving, Dunlawton was ravaged by Seminoles following the defeat of Florida troops under Benjamin Putnam in 1836. John Marshall of Louisiana purchased the property from the Andersons and rebuilt the mills in 1849. He successfully operated them until the mid-1850s.

Nassau County, which contained the port of Fernandina at the mouth of the St. Marys River, was also another area that proved alluring to planters. Although Fernandina had enjoyed a brief period of growth and notoriety in the early 1800s, it had slipped back into its traditional role of a small fishing village. The failure of Fernandina to mature into a major port did not stop planters from moving to the area. Amelia Island and the surrounding marshes attracted a number of settlers from Georgia and South Carolina. Emphasizing the cultivation of rice over all other crops, planters used slave labor to carve out drainage and irrigation canals in the tidal marshes. Sea island cotton was also a major cash crop, and by 1845, dependence on slave labor accounted for a black majority population.

The area along the St. Johns River initially attracted the interest of planters. Near the site of Jacksonville, Francis Philip Fatio, a Swiss immigrant, established his plantation, New Switzerland; his son-in-law, George Fleming, who had arrived in Florida near the end of the second period of Spanish control, built Hibernia on the opposite side of the river. Both the Fatio and Fleming families cultivated rice and sea island cotton throughout the antebellum period. Both families would also play important roles in the politics of Florida during the same period and down to the 20th century.

Red Banks was another second Spanish period plantation near Jacksonville. Originally owned by Francis Flora, the land passed to William Craig in 1799; Craig sold the plantation to Isaiah C. Hart, who sold it in 1830 to Isaacs Hendricks. A leading citizen of antebellum Jacksonville, Hendricks kept the plantation for 18 years before selling it to Albert Gallatin Phillips in 1848. In 1854 the current manor house was built from bricks produced on the plantation. The property was eventually sold to Hiram H. Palmer, the superintendent of public instruction for Duval County. In the 20th century, a real estate company subdivided the property into lots for homes.

Chapter Eight

CENTRAL AND SOUTH FLORIDA PLANTATIONS

With the conclusion of the Treaty of Moultrie Creek in September 1823 in which Seminole leaders agreed to move to a four million acre reservation between Charlotte Harbor and Ocala, the threat of Indian warfare seemed to have abated in Central Florida. The rolling hills of Alachua and Marion Counties attracted the attention of planters, and a number began to claim plantations in the area. Gen. Duncan Clinch was an early settler in region, and his Auld Lang Syne plantation, which was dedicated to the production of sugarcane, was some 10 miles south of Micanopy. Moses Elias Levy, who received a grant of 36,000 acres from the Spanish government and who had purchased an additional 52,900 acres, also began sugar operations in the region.

Although the peace guaranteed by the Treaty of Moultrie Creek was soon shattered as Seminole leaders resisted efforts to relocate them to the reservation or to transport them westward to Arkansas and Oklahoma, planters nevertheless continued their migration to Central Florida. A territorial land office was opened in Newnansville in 1843, and by 1845 some 5,500 acres had been purchased. Although the continued

conflict of the Seminole War certainly had a detrimental effect on the rapidity of white movement into Central Florida, the rate of settlement might have been faster had not complications arisen from the question of whether or not the Arredondo Grant was valid. The King of Spain gave the Duke of Alagon 290,000 acres of Alachua County land in February 1818, but the date of the grant was two weeks after the deadline was recognized as valid by the United States in the Adams-Onis Treaty. Richard S. Hackley purchased the Duke's claim in May 1819 and filed for confirmation of his title by the claims board created for that purpose, and the claim was granted in 1832. Subsequent litigation over the date the grant was issued kept the matter in various courts until January 1905, when the United States Supreme Court finally ruled it invalid. Once Central Florida was opened to settlement, Alachua County attracted a large number of settlers from South Carolina and other states in the Lower South.

Although there were hundreds of planters who prospered outside of the five-county Middle Florida plantation belt, they were not as successful or generally as wealthy as those in the counties immediately surrounding Tallahassee. Additionally, they failed to wield as much political or economic power. Only one planter from Alachua County, Madison Starke Perry, managed to break the stranglehold on the governor's chair that had been held since 1845 by planters from Middle Florida. By 1857, however, Alachua and Marion Counties had been fully integrated into the Middle Florida orbit. While they may have felt underrepresented in many areas, planters in the newer area of settlement were members of an elite class and shared a common set of values with their colleagues in the older plantation regions.

The ranks of the planter class, despite the influx of large numbers of aristocratic and wealthy individuals from other states, was to a large degree composed of men and women who had reached their exalted position, not by right of birth or inheritance, but by virtue of hard work and industry. The open lands of the Florida peninsula were available for the taking or for a minimal investment of money and a large helping of ability and hard work. To some degree, the same thing was happening throughout the newer states of the Lower South.

One of the earliest settlers in the county was James B. Bailey, who acquired a large number of acres within the original limits of Gainesville. Bailey was instrumental in persuading the legislature to move the county seat from Newnansville to Gainesville in 1852, a move that added considerable value to his property. In 1854 Bailey constructed a substantial but not ostentatious frame house that incorporated elements of the Greek-revival style.

The Haile family, led by Thomas Evans Haile of Camden, South Carolina, migrated to Alachua County in 1854. His brother, Edward; his mother, Amelia; and his brother-in-law, Thomas Chesnut, soon followed him to Alachua County. Members of prominent South Carolina families (the Haile brothers had married into the Gen. James Chesnut family, whose wife, Mary Boykin Chesnut, achieved some degree of fame for her *Diary From Dixie*), the Haile clan purchased large tracts of land from Henry Marquand, a land agent for owners of the disputed Arredondo Grant, and each set about carving plantations out of the wilderness. Large slave owners in South Carolina, the group brought more than 300 slaves with them when they came to Florida and set about producing crops of sea island cotton.

Thomas Haile and his wife, Ester Serena, had five children when they moved to Florida, and evidently Florida was conducive to growing families since 10 more children were born in their plantation home, Kanapaha. Slave laborers built Kanapaha, and the modest home included dormitory rooms for the children and a schoolroom for their education. The main house had a detached kitchen nearby, which was separated from the main house to protect against fires. The house and kitchen were surrounded by 18 slave cabins.

The cotton operations at Kanapaha were very successful. In the 1860 Census, Thomas Haile's plantation was valued at $15,000 and his personal estate, including slaves, at $45,000. While this placed him squarely in the ranks of the upper middle range of Florida planters, his mother, Amelia, was listing as having property worth $17,000 and a personal estate of $114,000. This made her the richest planter in the county, and her personal estate was almost double that of her nearest competitor, fellow South Carolinian G.O. Leitner, whose personal estate was $60,000. Leitner's property, however, was valued at $65,000; nearly four times the value of Amelia's plantation.

A strong supporter of secession and the Confederacy, Thomas Haile participated in the war as an officer in John J. Dickison's cavalry troop, while his oldest son, John, served as a private. When the Civil War ended, Haile returned to Kanapaha to grow cotton. A disastrous harvest, brought about by unusually heavy rains and an infestation of caterpillars, forced him to declare bankruptcy in 1868. His brother, Edward, who had established a successful mercantile business in Gainesville, purchased Kanapaha and some 40 surrounding acres. In 1873 the home and 110 acres were conveyed by deed to Ester Serena Haile and has remained in the possession of her descendants since then.

Participants in a turn-of-the-century outing at Kanapaha plantation pose for a photograph. The plantation has been fully restored and is now open to the public as a museum and visitor's center.

Elias Earle, a former brigadier general of the South Carolina Militia, came to Alachua County in 1858 and established his plantation on the west side of Lake Santa Fe. Two years later the census listed his wealth at $8,000 in real estate and $33,000 in personal wealth. Although a small-scale planter by the prevailing standards of the day, Earle nevertheless was able to afford a comfortable life in his foursquare Georgian home.

John and Maria Taylor settled south of Kanapaha in Marion County in 1854 with some 60 slaves. Originally from Beaufort, South Carolina, the Taylors purchased 1,300 acres for the cultivation of cotton. Giving their plantation the name Osceola, they prospered on the Florida frontier. Their 3,000-acre plantation in South Carolina, Myrtle Hill, had been valued at $11,000, and the 1850 Census placed the number of slaves they owned at 68. The smaller Florida plantation was valued at $16,000 in 1860, while John Taylor's personal estate was valued at $50,000. Osceola was typical of the kind of plantation home that central planters erected, and there is a similarity between it and Kanapaha in Alachua County. A single-roofed porch extends across the entire front of the two-story frame building. Modest in appearance and decidedly different from the more grandiose plantation homes of Middle Florida, Osceola blended into the surrounding environment.

In nearby Columbia County, small plantations dedicated to producing mixed crops of cotton, tobacco, and grains also began to emerge. In 1851 Noble A. Hull moved from Georgia to Florida, where he started a successful mercantile business. In 1853 his father, Joseph Hull, received a grant of a large tract of land from the federal government. On this property, now in Suwannee County, Noble Hull began to cultivate the 1,580 acres that made up the Hull grant. In the early 1860s he employed local craftsmen to build a suitable house for his family. The result is one of the best examples of "Carpenter Classic" architecture in existence in the state today. The style derives its name because no architect was involved in designing the structure or with supervising its construction. A simple hand-drawn sketch or a page from an architectural pattern book, popular during the period, provided a general guide for the carpenter, but he exercised considerable latitude in making alterations and resolving problems.

In 1842 Col. Byrd Pearson of Columbia, South Carolina, purchased a large tract of land in what was to become Hernando County in 1843. (In 1844 the county's name was changed to Benton County to honor Sen. Thomas Hart Benton of Missouri, who had supported the Armed Occupation Act of 1842. The name was changed back to Hernando County in 1850 when Floridians disagreed with Benton's moderate stand on the Missouri Compromise.) Here he established his Mount Airy plantation, which was given over to the production of cotton, citrus, and cattle. In 1852 Francis Higgins Ederington of Fairfield, South Carolina, purchased Mount Airy and continued to farm the property. Ederington also harvested cedar logs from nearby forests and shipped them to Germany until this trade was interrupted by the Civil War. He died in 1866. The Ederington family continued to own the property until 1904, when Raymond Robins purchased the property.

Robins renamed the property Chinsegut Hill and lived there with his wife until 1932 when he donated the plantation to the federal government for use as a wildlife refuge. During the Robins residency, many luminaries and government dignitaries visited the plantation, including Thomas A. Edison, John C. Penney, Harold L. Ickes, and others. The University of Florida operated the facility as a library and agricultural research facility for a number of years before transferring the property to the University of South Florida. It currently serves as a retreat for university conferences and was placed on the National Register of Historical Places in November 2003.

Not all planters who moved to the southern frontier were transplants from other states. In 1844 Robert Gamble, a prominent Middle Florida planter, placed the management of Welaunee, his large plantation in Jefferson County, in the hands of his son, Robert H. Gamble, and claimed some 3,500 acres in Manatee County, south of Tampa. With a force of 100 slaves, Gamble soon had a large cane crop planted and had constructed several large and substantial outbuildings to grind and cook the cane into sugar and molasses.

In 1888 Robert H. Gamble recalled the experience of living on the frontier and trying to make a new plantation profitable for the *Tallahassee Floridian*. Despite experiencing several turns of bad luck—such as a fire in 1849 that destroyed some 80,000 pounds of sugar and 4,000 gallons of molasses, and a devastating freeze in 1851–1852—Gamble soon began to produce crops that averaged 249,720 pounds of sugar and 10,900 gallons of molasses over the next six years. He also cut timber from the surrounding forest and shipped logs to New Orleans, Key West, and New York. In 1859 he sold this plantation to two planters from Louisiana for $190,000, who soon lost it because of raids by Union forces and the eventual abolition of slavery.

In 1842 Dr. Joseph Braden and his brother, Hector, gained title to some 1,000 acres of land in Manatee County and moved their slave force south to carve a new sugarcane plantation out of the wilderness. By 1845 a dozen plantations were producing hundreds of thousands of pounds of sugar and tens of thousands of gallons of molasses for the New Orleans market.

Opposite: The Gamble mansion was renovated in the 1940s. The classic "plantation house" look, featuring an avenue of tropical palms, showed the adaptability of this style of architecture to virtually any locale.

Above: The Gamble mansion still stands today. Note the shed roof to the extreme right of the main house. This covered a cistern that, when filled with rainwater run-off from the roof of the main house, provided a source of potable water and ensured a constant source during periods of drought. Many other houses in Florida, both urban and rural, featured a similar system of rainwater collection since sources of fresh water were sometimes hard to find and because of extended periods of little to no rainfall to replenish the aquifer.

The Gamble mansion, shown *c.* 1930, stood abandoned for a number of years before it was purchased by the United Daughters of the Confederacy and turned into a national monument honoring Judah P. Benjamin, who stayed there on his way to Cuba after the collapse of the Confederacy.

Chapter Nine

URBAN ANTEBELLUM HOMES AND THE PEOPLE WHO OWNED THEM

As Florida's plantations developed, so too did the small towns and villages in their midst. Merchants, bankers, industrialists, and such professionals as doctors, ministers, and lawyers, found a ready market for their services and goods, as did government employees who ensured that the day-to-day business were taken care of. In some cases, the dividing lines between planters and non-planters were blurred, as planters became bankers or industrialists or as merchants and ministers moved in and out of each other's professions. Some professionals who arrived in antebellum Florida became enamored with the status and prestige accorded wealthy planters and worked assiduously to become planters. The ever-changing Florida frontier (despite its veneer of Old South culture, Florida remained a boundary with fully two-thirds of the state sparsely settled by whites or completely under the control of Native Americans), presented the fluidity that made movement from class to class possible.

When the United States acquired Florida from Spain in 1821, there were only two towns of any consequence. St. Augustine in East Florida was a small village of a few hundred souls, while Pensacola in West Florida was even smaller and consisted of little more than derelict wooden houses and a few unpretentious government buildings. Between St. Augustine and Pensacola was almost 500 miles of unsettled land, dotted here and there with a few Catholic missions and Native American villages. Within a decade, however, a number of towns took root and, as the population grew, began to offer a modest respite from the rural isolation of small farms and plantations. As Middle Florida became the center of the plantation economy, St. Augustine and Pensacola became increasingly less important. Neither city offered much support for the burgeoning cotton and tobacco economy since they were off the major transportation routes, and both towns became little more than backwaters of Florida.

New towns, such as Tallahassee, St. Marks, Apalachicola, and Magnolia—connected to Middle Florida by rivers and rudimentary railroads—monopolized the commerce of the state, while Gainesville and Ocala, which developed in the late 1840s and 1850s, gained a growing importance when steam-powered railroads linked them to Atlantic and Gulf ports. Jacksonville, at the mouth of the St. Johns River, began to grow in the 1850s in response to both the development of the timber and naval stores industries in northeast Florida and the cotton and rice plantations along the river's banks. Jacksonville and Baldwin, some 20 miles to the west, became major railroad hubs and linked the interior of Florida with ocean-going vessels on the St.

Johns. Steam power pushed sidewheelers and sternwheelers up the wide river as far south as modern Brevard County. Even Fernandina, which had lain dormant for almost three decades, began to come alive in the 1850s as the Florida Railroad stretched into the interior of the state.

When Tallahassee became the capital of Florida, there was no town as such in Leon County. Built on the "Old Fields" of an Indian village, it amounted to little more than an odd assortment of shops and homes, most of which were fashioned from crudely dressed logs, that had the appearance of being exactly what it was—a new town carved out of a wild frontier. In 1845, however, urban renewal came to the town in the form of a devastating fire that destroyed the heart of the town. Coinciding with the opening of the new capitol building and Florida's entry into the Union, the fire provided an opportunity to start over and construct substantial buildings that were in keeping with the town's new status. Within a few years, plantations that once had

been regarded as far removed from the town were now included in its outskirts and after a few more years were incorporated into the town itself.

The prevailing architectural style of the urban elite houses in the "new" capital generally included elements from the Georgian style—largely preferred by the wealthiest of planters—and elements from the neo-Classical style that dominated government buildings. That is to say, the architecture of Tallahassee and the other towns of Middle Florida reflected the taste of the dominant planter class. Indeed, some planters maintained homes on their plantations and in town, while others built their manor houses in the towns and erected much smaller and less expensive houses on their plantations. The close proximity of Middle Florida plantations to towns made it difficult to discern any distinctive differences in architectural styles. The close social, economic, and familial relationships between urban elites and planters further blurred any differences.

Depicted here is the city of St. Augustine during the antebellum period.

In the early 1850s Peres Bonney Brokaw of New York purchased a portion of the Lafayette Grant in Leon County and built his two-story Greek-revival home near the center of Tallahassee in 1856. The house was surrounded by formal gardens that had been planted before the house was built. The small room at the center of the roof was a vent for hot air and was a critical element in cooling the house.

A successful livery operator, Peres Brokaw was also active in local and state politics. During the Civil War Brokaw served in the Confederate cavalry. His daughter married a Scottish immigrant, Alexander McDougall, and the house remained in the family's possession until 1973 when it was sold to the State of Florida.

Quincy, in Gadsden County, was home to Philip A. Stockton, an attorney who had come to Florida in 1836 with his brother, William, to establish and manage a stagecoach line between St. Augustine and Mobile, Alabama. Although the brothers originally established their headquarters in Marianna, they moved the operation to Quincy around 1840. Philip Stockton purchased a house that Isaac R. Harris had started, but not finished. Stockton completed the needed work on the house and moved his family sometime in 1843. A wonderful example of Classic-revival architecture, the Stockton home remained in family hands until 1902.

The small law office located behind the Stockton House was designed in the classic Greek-revival style that dominated antebellum architecture in Florida. From here, Philip A. Stockton conducted a lucrative legal practice, met with local political leaders, and engaged in an active social life.

An even more impressive antebellum home in Quincy is the house of Pleasants W. White, a local attorney and judge. White purchased the house from Joseph Leonard Smallwood, who had moved to Quincy in 1842 and completed the construction of the house in 1843. Smallwood also owned a plantation in rural Gadsden County and lived in the house during the winter months when planting activities had ceased. In 1849 Smallwood moved to New York and sold his town home to White. White's wife was a niece of Smallwood's, so the family tie was maintained.

During the Civil War, White served as the chief Confederate commissary agent in Florida, and since Quincy was a major supply depot, he probably spent a large part of his time at home. White also continued to practice law during his service to the Confederacy and after the war was appointed a judge of the newly created Second Judicial Circuit of Florida. He served a four-year term as the commissioner of land and immigration from 1881 to 1885.

Pleasants W. White died in 1919 and ownership of the house passed to his unmarried daughters, Rebecca and Jennette. They in turn sold the house to the Methodist Church in 1921 for use as a parsonage.

Another wealthy planter who maintained a home in Quincy was Roderick K. Shaw, who also served as a member of the legislature. In 1850 Shaw purchased a piece of property that had been the site of an earlier home for local schoolteacher Susan S. Snell. Whether or not Shaw razed the Snell home or incorporated it into an expanded home is unknown. What is known is that the Shaw House, now known as the E.C. Love House, took on its present configuration during 1850. Shaw lived in the house until 1860, when it was sold to William E. Kilcrease, another cotton and tobacco planter in the area. In 1874 E.C. Love, a local attorney and politician, purchased the property, and it has remained in the Love family since then.

Marianna served as the county seat for Jackson County. Home to a number of large plantations, Marianna had a large and thriving commercial district during the antebellum period. The homes of the merchants and professional people in the town were solid and typical of most small towns. The Holden House, built by Warren E. Anderson between 1849 and 1851, was the home of Dr. Julius Thomas Holden and was the main house for a small working plantation.

Apalachicola was an important town that profited from the transshipment of cotton and tobacco from the plantations in Jackson and Gadsden Counties, as well as plantations in western Georgia as far north as Columbus. During the 1840s Apalachicola was the third busiest port on the Gulf of Mexico and included 46 factors in residence.

The factors took cotton and tobacco on consignment from planters and made arrangements to sell their crops in New England or in Europe. Essential middlemen for plantation crops, factors also were a major source of credit for whatever needs planters might have. Frequently factors also served as "shoppers" for planters, purchasing furniture, furnishings, clothing, books, and whatever needs a planter family might have. The cost of such items was deducted from the proceeds of cotton and tobacco sales.

Above is the David G. Raney House in Apalachicola before renovations.

Few homes in smaller towns could match the Apalachicola home of David G. Raney, a prosperous merchant and manager of the Apalachicola Race Track. The exact date and place of construction of this home is not known. One story maintains that the Raney House was built in 1838 in nearby St. Joseph and moved to Apalachicola in 1841. St. Joseph experienced an outbreak of yellow fever that year , and a number of houses were moved from the afflicted region to Apalachicola. Another story has it that the home was constructed in Apalachicola in 1840. With the exception of a different order of columns supporting the front portico, the two-story Greek revival is almost identical to the home built by Edward C. Cabell in Tallahassee in 1855.

David G. Raney was an important local political leader. The Apalachicola militia unit, a source of political support, drills on the adjacent lot at the Raney House, *c*. 1890.

In Jefferson County, Walter Lloyd, an enterprising merchant, offered the Pensacola and Georgia Railroad three and a half acres of land for the purpose of erecting a depot, loading platform, and railroad yards. When the railroad accepted his offer, he immediately began to map out a complete town on nearby property that he and his wife owned. Thus was born the village of Lloyd.

Walter Lloyd had first arrived in the area in 1847 and had moved two small log cabins to form a permanent residence. It was around this house that the village of Lloyd blossomed, and for a number of years merchants profited from supplying the railroad and surrounding plantations with merchandise.

Adjacent Madison County also had a strong and vibrant community of merchants and professionals. One of the most prominent members of the community was Benjamin F. Wardlaw, who, although not a planter, enjoyed a great deal of popularity. A successful politician, he was a delegate from Florida to the Democratic conventions in Charleston and Baltimore in 1860. He also was a colonel in the Confederate Army during the Civil War, and after the war he continued to be active in local and state politics.

In February 1860 Wardlaw purchased property in downtown Madison, just two blocks west of the town's square, and hired local architect and builder William Archer Hammerly to design and build him a home. Although the house was not completed when he sold the property in November 1863, his name has remained attached to the house. The house is typical of the Classical-revival style, and its most notable architectural feature is the 20 columns that support the wide porches surrounding the home. It was restored by Mr. and Mrs. William Goza during the 1970s.

Madison was also home to Madison Livingston, who in 1836 built his house a few blocks north of the Wardlaw home. Livingston, who owned a sizeable bit of acreage, sold the first 160 acres of the town to the county commission. The Livingston home is considered the oldest extant home in Madison.

His son, Daniel G. Livingston, who was living in the house in 1865, is reported to have hosted Gen. John C. Breckinridge of the Confederacy and provided him with a fresh horse on his journey southward to escape arrest by Union soldiers.

Jacksonville, which had experienced a spurt of growth in the 1850s, also had a number of merchants and industries that catered to the plantation trade. One of the earliest settlers in the area was John S. Sammis, who came to Florida from New York in the 1820s. For a time he was employed by Zephaniah Kingsley. Sammis married one of Kingsley's daughters, Mary, and soon became an employee of Francis Richard, his brother-in-law, who operated a lumber mill near Jacksonville. When Richard died in 1839, Sammis purchased the mill and 5,000 acres of wooded land. By 1850 Sammis had acquired an estate with a cash value of $20,000. In 1860 he quit the lumber business and moved to Baldwin, a small town about 20 miles west of Jacksonville. The Sammis home on Fishcamp Bluff was probably constructed around 1838 by Oran Baxter, another relative by marriage. Sammis occupied the home soon after his purchase of the lumber mill. John Sammis was an ardent Unionist during the Civil War and moved back to Jacksonville, where in cooperation with other Unionists, he attempted to create an alternative government that was opposed to secession and war. In April 1864 John Sammis was chosen as a delegate to the Republican National Convention in Baltimore. He did not play a major role in Florida politics after the war but became involved in railroad construction. In 1870 Sammis moved to Mandarin and died there in 1884.

One of the most interesting antebellum houses in northeast Florida is the Merrick-Simmons House in Fernandina. It was probably built around 1856 by an unknown owner during the revival of Fernandina as a port city. The Direct Tax Commission seized this house in 1863 after its owner, a Confederate sympathizer, had abandoned it. Chloe Merrick, the Fernandina agent for the National Freedmen's Relief Association, purchased it in 1863. Eventually, Miss Merrick established a school and orphanage for emancipated slaves in the city. In 1869 she married Harrison Reed, the governor of Florida, and moved to Tallahassee.

South of Jacksonville was the small town of Middleburg, which had gained a measure of importance in the antebellum economy of Florida as an inland port and transshipment point for cotton, tobacco, and timber from the interior of the peninsula. In 1836 Fort Heileman, a supply depot for American troops during the Second Seminole War, made the town an important place of refuge for settlers fleeing Indian raids to the south. Gens. Winfield Scott and Thomas Jesup used the fort as their headquarters at various times during the war.

The Clark-Chalker House in Middleburg, shown here, is thought to have been constructed around 1835 as living quarters for Capt. Michael M. Clark, the army quartermaster. Fort Heileman was abandoned in 1841, and in 1845 Isaac Varnes bought the old fort from the federal government, including what was described as the "old Army hospital," which in all likelihood was the Clark residence. There is some evidence that the building then became a school for planter's children.

In 1859 William Sims Bardin purchased the property as a town residence. Middleburg was a prosperous village in the 1850s and counted two hotels, two drugstores, a school, nine general stores, two taverns, two ferries, three churches, a grocery store, and two coopers among its businesses. Bardin, who owned a large cotton warehouse adjacent to one of the ferries in addition to his large plantation outside of town, found his new home convenient for supervising this business.

During the Civil War, Sims, a veteran of the Second Seminole War, enlisted in the Florida Reserves and fought in Clay County. Middleburg's location on Black Creek, a major tributary of the St. John's River, made the town an inviting target for federal soldiers, and both Union and Confederate units swept through the area several times during the course of the war. Confederate troops were welcomed by the residents who remained in the town, but Union soldiers were feared because they frequently plundered stores and homes. On several occasions Union troops set fire to military stores and contraband, which threatened the entire town.

Although the Bardin home was pillaged several times, it escaped structural damage during the war. On Christmas Day 1865 the home became the scene of a wedding between Bardin's daughter, Martha Anne, and Albert Symington Chalker, a young man she had met while he was on duty with J.J. Dickison's Second Florida Cavalry. Bardin gave the house to the young couple as a wedding present and continued to live with them until his death in 1880. Albert Chalker was an ambitious young man who engaged in several business enterprises after the war. He owned the first private ferry to be chartered in the post-war period and operated that business from late 1865 until 1884. He also opened a successful general store, which was passed along to his son, George, upon his death in 1886. In addition to his business ventures, Chalker served as the town's postmaster and was a justice of the peace from 1881 to 1885.

In Palatka, Judge Isaac Bronson and his family built an imposing house, Sunny Point, which became a center for the community's social activities. Bronson, a U.S. Circuit Court judge, moved to Palatka from St. Augustine to oversee the bankruptcy of Robert Raymond Reid Jr. and other investors in the "Pilatka Tract." Barely two years after his arrival in Palatka, Judge Bronson died, but his widow Sophronia continued to live there until she returned to her home state of New York around 1860. During the Civil War, Sunny Point remained empty, but both Confederate and Union troops occupied it at various times. After the war Charlotte J. Henry bought the property and attempted to establish a freedmen's school there. Because of threats, the school soon folded. In 1904 the property passed to her nurse, Mary Mulholland.

Antebellum Pensacola was little more than a collection of wooden houses surrounding a large harbor.

One Pensacola merchant who did prosper during the antebellum period was George Barkley, who with his wife, Clara, arrived in the city in 1835. Barkley initially opened a "reading room" that specialized in the latest commercial information, which he gradually expanded into the mercantile business. A man with strong moral principles, he became a leading citizen of Pensacola through his advocacy of the promotion of "public morals, the diffusion of education, and the relief and comfort of the poor and needy." His home, as painted by local artist E.D. Chandler, was typical of upscale residences in antebellum Pensacola. (Pace Library, University of West Florida.)

Apalachicola, above, and Magnolia, below, were typical of the new towns that grew up overnight to service the commercial needs of Florida's planters. (Alma Clyde Field Library.)

Dock.   Signal Station.   Methodist Church.   Railroad Dock.
Baptist Church.   Yulee's House.

Fernandina, which had lain dormant for almost three decades, began to come alive in the 1850s as the Florida Railroad stretched into the interior of the state. Sea island cotton and naval stores provided Fernandina merchants with a profitable livelihood and encouraged the development of this small town. The construction of Fort Clinch nearby also gave it additional importance. (Alma Clyde Field Library.)

Antebellum Tallahassee, before the fire of 1845, was little more than a crude rural village of muddy streets, log cabins, and ugly frame houses. Within a decade, Tallahassee would be home to stately homes, brick commercial establishments, and impressive government buildings.

One of the most elegant town houses in Tallahassee was the Thomas Hagner House, built in 1843 just a few blocks from the new capitol. Hagner was an attorney from Virginia who was also a nephew of Thomas Randall. Randall himself was a Virginia lawyer who entered the planter ranks when he married the daughter of William Wirt of Jefferson County in 1827 and received a wedding present of 1,000 acres of cotton land from his new father-in-law. Wirt was married to a sister of John and Robert Gamble, who were among the wealthiest of the planter elite. Thomas Hagner also married into the Gamble family, thus assuring himself a close connection to high society.

The Hagner House, now known as the Knott House after later owner William V. Knott, was probably built by George Proctor, a free black contractor in Tallahassee. Originally, the house had six rooms and a side hall, but in 1853, it was enlarged by the addition of six more rooms. The Hagner-Knott House has played an important role in the history of Tallahassee. In 1865 Union Gen. Edward M. McCook used the house as his headquarters and read the Emancipation Proclamation on its front steps, a ceremony that is reenacted each year. Purchased in 1883 by Dr. George Betton, it was also the home of three Florida Supreme Court justices before being sold to the Knott family in 1928.

Another of Tallahassee's prominent residents, Edward Carrington Cabell, who also owned the Dulce Domum plantation in Jefferson County, built his home in Tallahassee in 1855. Although he was a planter, Cabell was also an active Whig politician who served several terms as a congressman. He became the president of the Pensacola & Georgia Railroad in the 1850s. The Cabell House was a fixture in Tallahassee until it was torn down in 1948. A furniture store replaced this stately mansion.

Chapter Ten

CRACKER HOMES ON FLORIDA'S FRONTIER

There was another style of architecture that existed in antebellum Florida. Despite the dominance of planters and their urban allies, the simple fact was that the majority of the population in pre–Civil War Florida was made up of common people—laborers or yeoman farmers and their families. Laborers in towns and villages found competition with slave labor disheartening, and the absence of large amounts of specie made it extremely difficult for a wage-based economy to flourish. Generally, they lived miserable lives of poverty, made more difficult by the ups and downs of the cotton and tobacco markets. Skilled workmen fared somewhat better, but they still faced the specter of competition from slaves and the vacillations of the plantation economy. Not much is known about the daily lives of these individuals, because they left few records behind and because the dwellings they occupied were generally modest to begin with and poorly maintained.

The largest group in antebellum Florida was yeoman farmers and their families, who struggled to eke a subsistence living on the frontier. Unable to muster the financial resources to acquire large tracts of land and to acquire slaves, these individuals labored long hours to clear small patches of ground for food crops and occasionally produced enough cotton or tobacco to sell on the open market to bring small amounts of cash into family coffers. Hunting, fishing, and the judicious slaughter of domesticated animals supplemented their meager diets.

Yeoman farmers lived in houses that contained only the basics. Few examples of antebellum countrymen homes still exist, because they were replaced as soon as individuals acquired enough wealth to do so or abandoned as yeomen moved on in search of better land and lives elsewhere. Even the wealthiest of early planters lived in crude cabins that were little better than those of the countrymen who surrounded them. Many of these early cabins were incorporated into the larger manor houses and covered with dressed lumber or plaster.

Ronald W. Haase, a professor of architecture at the University of Florida, examined the design and construction of some of the earliest cabins in the state and identified two basic structures in his 1992 book *Classic Cracker: Florida's Wood-Frame Vernacular*

Architecture. The first is the so-called "single pen" cabin, which featured a single room, used for all purposes, surrounded by porches on all sides. The second was the "double pen." Easy to construct, a cabin could be erected in a matter of a few days. Undressed logs, many with the bark remaining, were set on a series of low pillars and notched on either end. The logs were then brought together to form the outer walls. A sloping gable roof, usually covered with shingles rived from cypress or cedar, extended out from the top row of timbers. A crude floor of "punched" planking would be used as a floor, while similar boards would be used to create a ceiling and an attic. Crudely split planking was used to make doors, while windows were usually nothing more than crude openings covered with fabric or wooden shutters. Such cabins were substantial buildings, designed to keep out the elements and to serve as a fortified refuge in the event of Native American attacks.

This "cracker" house, although constructed in the early 1900s, retains the shape, size, and look of earlier houses on the Florida cotton frontier. (Florida State Archives.)

This cabin in the Withlacoochee Forest was typical of cabins of small farmers and settlers outside of Florida's cotton belt.

Although this late 19th-century "Cracker" house in northern Florida is built with rough-sawn boards, the basic design is drawn from early to mid-1800 models. (Florida State Archives.)

Life on Florida's frontier was hard for everyone, but especially for women. In addition to cooking, child rearing, and the other chores that came with running a home, women were expected to tend the garden, care for the livestock, and assist with clearing fields. The average single-pen or dogtrot cabin, while not very big, offered very little in the way of aids to help with these jobs. (*Harper's New Monthly Magazine*, 1887.)

As planters and yeoman farmers garnered more and more wealth on the Florida frontier, they expanded their homes. Frequently, the old structures were incorporated into the new structures. The Joshua Davis home in Gadsden County was typical of such expansion. The large timbers of the original cabin were covered over. This is a view of the kitchen area during recent renovations.

Ed Birnhardt works to replace a door on the Joshua Davis House. Note the insulation stuffed between the dressed logs of the original cabin that makes up the heart of this house. Originally, the insulation would have most likely been Spanish moss mixed with mud and straw. Not only did this mixture provide insulation against the weather, but also it bound the various courses of logs together. This process is sometimes referred to as "chinking."

Cooking was both a necessity and a constant danger for early settlers. The constant heat of an open fireplace could make cabins uncomfortable during the summer months, while the need to keep a fire going 24 hours a day made fire a real hazard. As a result, most kitchens—in small cabins and large plantation manors—were usually detached from the main building.

These two gentlemen are "riving" shingles, a skill that was needed for roofing the many small cabins on Florida's frontier. Indeed, many of the larger and fancier homes of planters and merchants also had shingled roofs. Although these men were photographed in the 1930s, the technique remained the same. (Federal Land Reclamation Project, Withlacoochee-Hernando County.)

The Joshua Davis House is pictured in 1900. The use of sawn lumber and decorative columns could completely mask the humble origins of a house.

Although this single-pen cabin was built around 1875 in Volusia County, it provides a good example of one of the many variants of this design that were to be found in rural Florida during the 19th century. (Florida State Archives.)

This small frame house incorporates a high-pitched roof and is architecturally identical to the earlier single-pen log cabin of frontier Franklin County. It is elevated on wooden pilings to protect it from termites and to catch a cooling breeze. (Florida State Archives.)

Though difficult to recognize from the outside, the Joshua Davis House in Gadsden County was constructed around a single-pen cabin.

When homesteads had been cleared and crops planted, yeoman farmers could dedicate more time toward the construction of more elaborate homes. One of the most widely used designs was that of the "dog trot" cabin.

Initially, two simple cabins were constructed facing each other and separated by a 6- to 10-foot hallway. The two cabins were linked together by a commonly shared front and back porch and a common gable roof that united the two elements into a single structure. The hallway, referred to as the dogtrot, completed the process of integrating the various components into a whole. This style allowed occupants to gain the maximum benefits of the breezes that blew through the area, as well as providing a sense of privacy and separation. Eventually such simple two-roomed houses could be expanded to include four or six rooms for a minimum cost.

The dogtrot cabin, with its wide central hallway, was a feature of Florida architecture throughout the 19th century and well into the 20th century. Shown here is the John Wiley Hill homestead in Homeland, Florida. (Florida State Archives.)

This is a typical dog-trot cabin in the Ocala National Forest near Lake Kerr. (Florida State Archives.)

Out of the dogtrot cabin emerged the "four-square Georgian" house, with its four equal-sized rooms sharing the common hallway design of the dogtrot. This picture was taken at Kanapaha at the Haile Plantation in Alachua County.

A typical house in rural Florida in the early 1900s still retains many of the architectural elements of earlier single-pen and double-pen cabins. Many of these houses did not incorporate the "dog trot" hallway and the front door opened immediately into living space. (Federal Land Reclamation Project, Withlacoochee-Hernando County.)

The "L" house that was common to early Florida architecture was also a derivative of the dogtrot and single-pen cabins. Sometimes, a single house would incorporate elements of all styles. Once again, Kanapaha (Haile Plantation) is a good example. Although the house appears to be a simple Georgian from the front, the addition of several rooms in a line from the rear makes it an "L" house as well.

So, too, did the "I-house" design share a common heritage with the dogtrot cabin. Usually constructed as a simple "four-over-four" with a large central hallway and shared chimneys, the I-house was general much larger than the foursquare Georgian. The additional square footage comes from the addition of two or three rooms, built in a line, that extended from the rear of the main structure. This footprint gives the style its distinctive name.

A separate gabled roof covered these rooms and an additional shared chimney and double-facing fireplaces provided heat. Once again, the home's kitchen was usually detached from the main structure. The two views of Kanapaha prior to renovations show the extension of living space from the main house structure to the original kitchen structure located at the far right.

139

The Marjorie Kinnan Rawlings house in Cross Creek illustrates how an "I" house developed architecturally. The small front portion of the house, derived from the design of a double-pen cabin, is added to as the need arises by the simple technique of adding rooms in a line at the back.

Epilogue

Florida was an unusual place for the development of a stable Old South society. Abandoning its Spanish and British colonial heritage of a cultural backwater of 4,000 to 5,000 European inhabitants, Florida moved rapidly from a rough-and-tumble frontier in 1821 to a mature society of some 140,000 white and black residents by 1860. The 78,679 white residents came by choice, mostly to take advantage of the opportunities for achieving great wealth or for moving up in society. The 61,745 black residents came as slaves with no consideration given as to their individual desires. Despite ongoing wars with Native Americans for much of the antebellum period, the population of whites and blacks continued to grow each decade with no end in sight on the eve of the Civil War. Florida's society was dominated by a handful of slaveowners, who set the tone for the social and political activities of the state. So, too, did they dominate the state's economy. Their control of Florida was merely an extension of the control planters exercised in all of the states of the South. Around them emerged a supporting class of merchants and professional men, usually located in cities and towns, and a subservient class of yeoman farmers who struggled to establish their own niche in Florida society.

Four styles of construction dominated Florida architecture from the earliest frontier days until the end of the Civil War. Overall, they represented examples of clean designs, which provided the best use of available building materials at a reasonable cost, and which made use of design as the best means of cooling and heating large areas of space.

The availability of gas and electricity in the post-war years allowed for the construction of more elaborate designs of the Victorian period. Gas could provide light and heat artificially, and it also provided a safer means of cooking. Electricity could do all that, plus it could power fans to circulate air for cooling. Thus the center hallway, which distinguished the dogtrot cabin, the I-house, and the foursquare Georgian houses, was no longer needed. Rooms could be arranged in a variety of patterns without regard to the use of nature. The eventual development of air conditioning for home use spelled the death knell of these styles.

The basic designs used for housing during the first 40 years of American Florida endured because they met the basic needs of settlers at a reasonable or affordable price. Early cabins and houses, constructed of native material, were environmentally friendly structures that allowed residents to compensate for weather conditions through design features. The dogtrot, which allowed breezes to pass unhindered through houses, were retained as "entry halls" in more elaborate houses, but their function remained the same. Shared chimneys, high ceilings, and long windows were also found in the simplest cabins and the most elaborate homes. These were features common to the homes in many regions during the antebellum period, but which reached the greatest development and utilization in Florida. Many of these practical design features were ignored during the post-war years and much of the 20th century.

Interestingly, however, there has been an increased interest in reviving such designs in the last 25 years. Environmentally conscious homeowners wishing to conserve fossil fuel resources have returned to the simple, yet elegant, designs of early Florida. A few architects, such as Ronald Haase and John T. Parks, have sought to incorporate many of these features into their designs for modern Florida homes. Variations of the single pen, dogtrot, and foursquare designs are appearing throughout Florida in seaside communities, in gated subdivisions, and on individual lots.

It is ironic that what was once considered passé has again become popular.

Although this yeoman family came to Florida around 1890, their mode of travel, a two-wheeled wagon pulled by a team of oxen, was very similar to those conveyances used by settlers in the antebellum period. The large two wheels allowed the wagon to clear stumps and other obstacles. They also allowed the wagon to make sharp turns between trees—a necessity since there were few roads in the state until much later.

For Additional Reading

As is so often the case with coffee table books, *Florida's Antebellum Homes* merely scrapes the top of the information heap. We have used several important sources for information about antebellum Florida and its peoples. We recommend that the reader refer to these complete works to gain a greater understanding of the complexity of Florida's emergence as a plantation society.

Baptist, Edward E. *Creating and Old South: Middle Florida's Plantation Frontier Before the Civil War*. Chapel Hill and London: University of North Carolina Press, 2002.

Blakey, Arch Fredric and Ann Smith Lainhart and Winston Bryant Stephens, Jr., *Rose Cottage Chronicles: Civil War Letters of the Bryant-Stephens Families of North Florida*. Gainesville and other Florida cities: University Press of Florida, 1998.

Cardwell, Harold D. Sr. and Priscilla D. Cardwell, *Images of America: Port Orange*. Charleston: Arcadia Publishing, 2000.

——————. *Images of America: Ormond Beach*. Charleston: Arcadia Publishing, 1999.

——————. *Port Orange: A Great Community*. Port Orange: City of Port Orange, 2001.

Denham, James M. *A Rogue's Paradise: Crime and Punishment in Antebellum Florida, 1821–1861*. Tuscaloosa: The University of Alabama Press, 1997.

Haase, Ronald W. *Classic Cracker: Florida's Wood-Frame Vernacular Architecture*. Sarasota: Pineapple Press, 1992.

Knetsch, Joe. *Florida's Seminole Wars, 1817–1858*. Charleston: Arcadia Publishing, 2003.

Madgigine, Anna and Daniel L. Schafer. *Jai Kingsley: African Princess, Florida Slave, Plantation Slaveowner*. Gainesville and other Florida cities: University Press of Florida, 2003.

Paisley, Clifton. *The Red Hills of Florida, 1528–1865*. Tuscaloosa and London: The University of Alabama Press, 1989.

Schwartz, Kathryn Carlisle. *Baptist Faith in Action: The Private Writings of Maria Baker Taylor, 1813–1895*. Columbia: University of South Carolina Press, 2003.

Shofner, Jerrell. *Florida Portrait: A Pictorial History of Florida*. Sarasota and Tampa: Pineapple Press and The Florida Historical Society, 1990.

——————, *History of Jefferson County*. Tallahassee: Sentry Press, 1976.

Sims, Elizabeth H. *A History of Madison County, Florida*. Madison: Madison County Historical Society, 1986.

Ste. Claire, Dana. *Cracker: The Cracker Culture in Florida History*. Daytona Beach: The Museum of Arts and Sciences, 1998.